Magical:
An Anthology of
Fantasy, Fairy Tales,
and Other Magical
Fiction for Adults

Edited by Kelly Ann Jacobson

To the voices in my dreams, the dragons in my imaginings, the unlikely tales that grab ahold of me and won't let me go.
To the muse.
To the magic.

CONTENTS

ACKNOWLEDGMENTS

I would like to dedicate this book to my contributors, who inspired me daily with their creative works. Anthologies are always a labor of love, but getting the chance to put these stories into the world was a privilege. I wish all of the amazing writers great success in their careers, and hope that they are fulfilling, prosperous, and at least a little bit *Magical*.

1. THE CLOCKWORK GIRL
by T.A. Noonan

The Worshipful Company of Clockmakers agreed: Joseph was truly worthy of the title "Master." When Anthony, the previous Master, gave him a fist-sized crown gear and dared him to build something with it, no one believed that Joseph could.

Yet before them stood a marvel.

"Does it have a name?" they asked.

Joseph bristled at the way they referred to his daughter as *it*. "*She*. And yes, she does. Her name is Pina. Say hello, Pina."

The clockwork girl curtsied. "Hello, everyone."

"What we want to know," his colleagues said, "is why you put a dress on it. Seems like a waste of cloth."

"Because," he said, "a good father doesn't let his child run around naked."

They laughed.

"It's a doll! You can't call her your daughter. It isn't even real!"

Joseph took Pina's hand. He could feel her fingers—fine enough to pluck a single hair from a man's beard—twitch. "Then strike my name from the Guild. I will not have my child treated like a toy."

"Wait," they said. "Please reconsider. This thing is a masterpiece. No one's ever made anything like it."

"That you still call her 'it' shows that you don't respect her. And if you don't respect her, you don't respect me. Farewell."

As they left the Guild and returned home, Pina thought about what the men had said. "They said I'm not real, that I'm a doll and not your daughter. Is that true?" She looked at her father with wide, camera-like eyes. Her brass lashes fluttered, as if blinking back tears.

Joseph frowned. He knew he would have to have this talk with her someday; he just hadn't expected it to come so soon. "You know how I told you that you don't have a mother?"

"Uh huh."

"Well, most little girls have a mother and a father. But you're different. I made you without a mother."

"That means I'm not a real girl."

"No," he said. "It means you're different, nothing more. Here, let me show you."

Once they reached home, Joseph unlocked the door to his workshop and led her inside. He showed her schematics for her joints, diagrams of her face, the lovely crown gear at her heart. Pina heard phrases like "vertical escapement" and "hydraulic actuators" and "rotary motion," but she didn't understand any of it.

He saw her blinking slow, her golden jaw clench. "You're confused," he said. "I think it's time I sent you to school. You'll understand once you learn. It'll take time, but whenever you need help, you can ask me. I'm your father."

The next day, Pina walked to school alone, determined to understand everything her father had talked about. But as soon as she entered the yard, the other children stared. The staring continued as she moved to her classroom. Embarrassed, she chose a seat in the back, far away from her fellow students.

"Settle down, children," the blue-haired teacher said. "Now, if you'll turn your books to page forty-nine, we'll continue the story of the Pleiades—"

But even as she tried listening to her teacher, she couldn't help but overhear the other children:

"What is that?"

"Is that a girl?"

"Can't be—girls don't have skin like that."

"Did you see her eyes? They're made of glass!"

She remembered what the clockmakers said and felt ashamed. Everyone could tell she wasn't real. Though she went to school every day, heard every lesson, and saw every letter and number that the teacher scrawled onto the board, she didn't learn about *whatever escapement* or *rotary something*. Whenever her father queried her about school, she responded with unfocused eyes and silence. She never asked him a single question.

This went on for weeks, until one day, a group of three boys stopped her on her way to school.

"Hey," said the first, "I hate to break it to you, but real girls don't look like that. They wear makeup, all kinds of creams and powders." He removed his fists from bulging pockets and opened them to reveal a half-dozen tiny jars and compacts.

"Yeah," said the second, "and real girls don't walk like you do, either. They walk like this." He stuck his butt out, wiggled it back and forth with each step, and grinned, revealing perfect teeth.

"But the really real girls," said the third, "don't go to school. They skip to go to shows and wait for boys to take them home." He brushed his blond hair from his face and raised one crooked eyebrow. "We'll help you become a real girl. All you need to do is give us some money."

Pina thought for a moment. Her father gave her a little money every day, and he told her to save whatever she didn't spend. She had a lot of coins in her purse, perhaps too many to give to these boys. But then she remembered the people who came to her father's shop and exchanged those same coins for her father's work—his clocks, repairs, and advice. She realized these boys were like her father. They had knowledge and skills; they understood what she needed. Smiling, she handed her money to the boys.

"Now remember," said the first as he handed over the makeup, "you want to put that all over your face."

"Yes," said the second, "and really get that butt out when you walk."

"And check out the magic carnival on the other side of the city," said the third. "Just follow the red balloons and make sure to find a boy to take you home."

The three ran off, laughing and tossing her purse between them.

Pina found a window with a ledge where she could arrange the jars and compacts. Looking into the glass, she smeared glittery powders on her eyelids, pink cream blush across her cheeks, red pigment around her lips. Then, she carefully stuck her butt out and took a few wiggly steps in place. Feeling like a real girl at last, she headed down the road in the direction of the carnival.

But it wasn't long before she was uncomfortable. Her body wasn't built to walk so strangely, and she could feel the makeup dripping into the crevices of her face and neck. By the time she reached the carnival, she heard gears snapping, popping. The crown at her center clacked. She felt pain. Something was wrong.

Pina straightened up and began walking normally. The gear slipped back into place, but she could barely control the tremors in her limbs. Still, she moved slowly through the carnival, stopping at every tent, every performance. She marveled at the fire-eaters, the beautiful women behind lacy fans, and the contortionists whose bodies moved even more impossibly than the boy who had taught her how real girls walked.

At each show, she tried to catch boys' eyes, but not one paid her more than a confused glance. Her face stuck and froze more and more with each boy that passed. The tremors grew worse until she could barely keep her balance. Every part of her strained and clanged, and she realized, at last, that no boy was going to take her home.

Then, she thought of her father. How long had she been gone? Was he worried? Angry? Surely he would see the damage, dismantle her, and scrap her parts—including her beautiful crown-gear heart. She collapsed into the dirt and sobbed tearlessly.

"You shouldn't sit on the ground like that, clockwork girl. You'll get even more dirt into those gummed-up gears." A slender arm covered in a silver-geared gauntlet reached down and yanked her to her feet.

"Who are you?" Pina asked.

The woman towered into the black sky, her coiled hair and skirt almost floating around her. "I'm Lady Ashe. I keep people from ever wanting to leave this carnival."

"My name is Pina." She tried to curtsey, but her body shook so hard that she almost fell over. "Please help me. I'm hurt and need to get home."

Lady Ashe felt her heart soften but maintained a stone gaze. "I have no use for clockwork girls anyway. Very well. I'll let you go under one condition."

"Anything."

"Find the one known as Blue Fairy. Your journey will be painful, but you can't give up, no matter what happens. If you do, you'll return here, and I won't be able to save you."

"I'll find her. I promise."

"I think you will, clockwork girl." She placed a handkerchief embroidered with crickets into Pina's hand, closed the girl's fingers around it, and pointed to a cluster of stars. "Follow the Seven Sisters. When you find Blue Fairy, give her that. She'll understand. Now go!"

Pina nodded, locked her eyes on the stars, and started to run through the carnival. Even though she could feel every mechanism struggle, every joint shear, she didn't stop. Hands clawed her ankles, grabbed her dress, and tried to drag her back. Sweet voices sang her name, swore to give her everything she could ever want. She felt the whale-like carnival try to swallow her like a squid, but she resisted every temptation and twisted her way out of every grip. It felt like hours before she finally escaped its teeth, leaving a ghost of red balloons and glittery lights in the distance.

The path before her was deserted, stretching through forests, towns, and farms. Occasionally, she met people along the way, but she ignored them all, lest they distract her. As the days, weeks, and months wore on, she continued to follow the Seven Sisters as they moved across the sky. Each step was a struggle. The stress of walking so strangely had damaged her in ways she didn't understand; the makeup that she'd worn so long ago had worked itself through every part of her system. In time, it oozed into her eyes, blinding her so she could barely make out the stars she followed.

Then, one day, she felt her fingers give, and the handkerchief fell from her clenched fist. As she bent to pick it up, Pina remembered Lady Ashe's reproach—"you'll get even more dirt in those gummed-up gears"—and wondered if she could clean herself. Fighting the shaking pain, she unfolded the cloth and reached into her mouth. She had never done this, but she knew that if she took her time, she could do it. Calling on the memory of her father's diagrams and his delicate handiwork, as well as her own knowledge of her body's motion, she began to clear away the grime that had overtaken her.

As she finally worked her way toward the lenses of her eyes, she saw her blue-haired teacher standing before her.

"Dearest Pina," she said with a warm smile. "It's so good to see you again."

"Teacher, are you Blue Fairy?"

"Yes. And you've learned one of the most valuable lessons of all: how to be strong enough to take care of yourself." Blue Fairy reached out, took the handkerchief from Pina's hands, and swept the girl up in strong, supportive arms. "Now, let me teach you another—how to be strong enough to rely on others when you need it."

Blue Fairy carried her the rest of the way home. Joseph was so overjoyed to see his beautiful daughter that he didn't even notice her ruined clothes or filthy insides.

Over the next several days, Joseph and Blue Fairy, working together, restored her health and taught her everything about her body. Joseph helped Pina connect those strange phrases she'd heard so long ago—"vertical escapement," "hydraulic actuators," "rotary motion," and many others—to the sensations she'd experienced. Blue Fairy, meanwhile, helped Pina understand the world she'd experienced at the edge of her vision, places only seen in passing as she'd stared at stars.

It took time, but Pina had already learned what really mattered; the rest was extra.

When she was ready to build a life for herself, she kissed her father goodbye and returned to school one final time. Blue Fairy was gone. Another teacher had taken her place, and all that remained was the grease-stained handkerchief resting on her former desk. Pina tucked it into her pocket and left her home behind.

Once she settled down, she no longer felt the need to be anything but a clockwork girl—no, a confident clockwork woman. As the years passed, she became a master clockmaker in her own right and a mentor to generations of girls struggling with their own realness. And no one—no boy or girl, man or woman—ever questioned why she wore a dirty handkerchief around her head like a scarf. Even if they didn't know her story, they knew a badge of honor when they saw one.

2. BLUES
by Oliver Gray

He extended his arm, feeling every tendon and nerve shudder as he opened his fist. Raw energy—a supernatural blend of scalding hot and freezing cold—sloshed in his veins, built near his shoulder, crept toward the gnarled and scarred digits pointed at the target looming just outside his vision. Blurry, impossibly distant. His eyes narrowed as he lined the nail of his pointer finger up with the painted red dot in the center. A sharp inhale. A slow, deliberate exhale.

Just as he was silently recalling the arcane summons, mentally forcing all that power through his heart and to his arm, seconds before he was supposed to spray several perfect jets of flame across the room, he burped.

Instead of neat, searing darts, the fire escaped from his mouth in an explosive cloud of brimstone and sulfur. It billowed and rose, growing larger and hotter, until the entire vaulted ceiling of the academy's main chamber glowed orange and yellow, raining embers on all the wizards below. Tapestries caught the magical flames first, their millions of threads perfect little wicks for Amber's mistake. Before he could even close his mouth, the panicked faculty began to conjure any water they could to quell the belched inferno.

Magister Ol'rean sighed and passed his heavy silk-covered arm through the air. The drops fell slow at first, plunking off the brim of Amber's brown hat. The indoor monsoon splashed and clashed with the enchanted fire, hissing and kissing as they danced around the room in a steamy tango. The magister, only visible in the fog because of his bright red robes, walked slowly over to Amber, and said, without hesitation, "Get out."

Amber's real magic hadn't manifested until he was in his mid-thirties. As a child he'd felt isolated by his differences, ostracized by the other children because of his ability to stay warm in his underclothes during a blizzard, or his penchant for knowing exactly what someone was about to say a second before they said it. But despite the hints and flirtation with the mystical, he never overtly displayed any signs of true magical power until the beard on his face (and callous on his soul) had grown thick.

By the time he'd recognized that he could refill a bucket of water just by yelling at it, or that he could carry on complete but very boring conversations with chickens, he did not qualify for traditional schooling. The Academy had never hosted such an old acolyte, and many assumed Amber could not be trained, nor broken of his human habits that made him an unpredictable, if not dangerous, wielder of magic.

Amber liked to drink. A lot. As a child his father would slip him ale in the tavern. Putrid stuff, really, but more than capable of sending a child's mind swimming in a sea of giggly glee. As he got older, he moved on to more spirited tinctures, eventually finding a way to spike them with natural magic for that little extra oomph.

But even a trained potion master was forbid from dabbling in mind altering substances. Magic, with all its glory and majesty, also carried the potential for destruction and corruption when used inappropriately. Rule Four of the Wizard code stated that "no wizard shall voluntarily lose control of his faculties, nor poison his mind or spirit with chemical or spell." Amber violated this rule daily, brewing batches of sour bishop beer in his tiny room, downing gulp after gulp of homemade eldritch gin.

It was that same potent gin ambling drunkenly through his system the day of his trials. He'd practiced. He'd perfected. He'd promised himself he would not drink that morning. But when faced with a room of fifty elders and the grand magus himself, he'd thrown back several swigs just to steady his arm.

The physical disaster was bad enough (the grand hall looked like a war scene), but the emotional aftermath was even worse; his trial had

8

been the last of the day, and he'd watched several 13 year olds pass all four elemental challenges without trouble. His best friend, Deema, had transformed a pile of rocks into an animated body guard and earned her blue robes. Amber still wore his dingy brown acolyte garb, having never even come close to passing the basic tests to prove his mastery of the raw elements.

He shuffled through the door and stood in the corner, watching the stewards mop up puddles of water and pull the charred tapestries down from the sooty walls. The magister noticed, but did not attempt to speak to him. He hung his head, awaiting his lecture, punishment, or presumably, both.

After a few minutes, Ol'rean waved Amber over without making eye contact. Several of the younger stewards glared at him as he passed, mocking him with their eyes, blaming him for this early morning emergency cleaning job. He wanted to apologize, help them clean, but he knew a wizard was not meant to socialize with the non-magical staff. He took off his still damp hat and crumpled it against his chest.

Ol'rean had changed robes, and he stood before Amber in a blaze of authority. "I'm not going to mince words. You're going to be removed from the school. We can't just let you terrorize the countryside with your loose magic either, so you'll be null-shackled and probably monitored by an elder. I can't give you any more chances, Amber. Not after the goat-dragon transmogrification incident. This was it, your last test, and you failed."

His gasp was interrupted by tears. He'd expected punishment, maybe several hours banishing imps from the library, or cleaning the falcon droppings off the observatory dome, but not full expulsion. Not shackling. Not being collared like some disobedient dog. He wanted to be insulted, to argue, but the magister was right. He'd blown more chances than should have ever been given. Amber had only himself to blame for the mistakes and accidents, and if the Academy couldn't train him, they'd have to control him.

"Do you have anything to say?" asked Ol'rean, letting some of the sternness drop out of his voice.

Amber looked up, eyes glistening like the water on the marble floor.

"No...sir. I just...no. I'm sorry. I wish I'd never found my magic."

Ol'rean put an arm on his shoulder, like a father comforting his son. "It's not an easy burden to bear, being magical, and nature did you no favors. You tried. I tried. We all tried. You can still be happy—like you were before the Academy—we'll just have to be…cautious."

With that, Ol'rean held out his arm. Amber draped his hat, sash, and cover-robe over the embroidered red silk, reaching for the broken hunk of ash he'd been using as his staff. "No," the magister said, "you keep that. With the shackle it won't work anyway, but it may be a good reminder of who you are."

Amber waited in his room, spinning a small glass around on the tip of his finger, balancing it with simple wind magic. He'd sipped, then swallowed, then gulped, then chugged when he'd returned, knowing that as soon as the keymaster arrived, they'd fit his new fashion accessory. No more magical drinks, no more easy brewing fires.

A zap, like a lightning bolt splitting the air right next to his head, caused Amber to jump up out of bed, lose concentration, and send the glass tumbling to the stone floor. He barely heard the glass shatter as shouts from the hallway mixed with the undeniable sound of magic colliding with magic.

His head spun, and he struggled to maintain his balance. He clutched his little staff close, too drunk to be truly scared, but still apprehensive about opening his door and peering into the hallway. Before he could even reach for the doorknob, Deema burst through the door, a splash of blood decorating her brand new cerulean robes.

"Amber! You've got to get out of here!" she said, her voice stained with pain and exhaustion, "Malg…he's back. He's captured all the elders in the main hall. You've got to run!"

He swayed, unsure he'd heard what he thought he'd heard. He looked at her through sad, sunken eyes, and fell back down onto his bed. "AMBER!" Her scream snapped him back to reality. "Are you drunk? For all that's mystical, pull yourself together. He'll kill you if he finds you here. Kill you…or worse." Her voice trailed off. "Just run. I'll hold him here."

Amber lurched forward and out the door. His steps were awkward and clumsy, the drink more in control of his limbs than his brain. He rushed down one hallway, then another, then another, unsure of where to go except away from all the cries and noise behind him. He turned a hard corner, lost his footing, and fell backwards through two large double doors.

From his back, looking upside down, he realized he'd run exactly the wrong direction and into the main chamber. He could see several elders, once encased in an eight inch-thick block of ice, another trapped mid-scream in some kind of time vortex. A pile of robes sprawled empty next to him, a tiny bump in it occasionally moving and making sounds remarkably similar to a croaking frog. As he started to realize that this was probably the worst room to be in at that exact moment, he saw Ol'rean, shoulder pierced with a large stone shard, hanging from the far wall.

Rolling back onto his knees, Amber called out, but the magister did not respond. The commotion in the hallway had died down, with only residual cracks of magical aftershock breaking the silence. As he pulled himself onto his feet, Amber realized he was not alone.

"What is this? The oldest acolyte in history? Ha! And intoxicated too, it seems." Malg wore the black and purple of the Northlands, the place of exiles, oathbreakers, and murderers. His cloak covered his eyes, but an eerie red glow filled the hood, and his yew staff pulsed and shuddered, tipped with a still-beating satyr's heart. Amber stood frozen, unsure whether to run or cry or beg. As Malg drew back his staff and lifted himself into the air, Amber covered his face with both arms and closed his eyes, trying to remember some spell, any spell.

Instead of his body filling with excruciating pain, Amber was knocked backwards into a giant rabbit; the first and only thing he could think to summon. The fur broke his fall, and the panicked, oversized animal started tearing around the room, knocking over braziers, leaping off of lecterns, eventually stopping to gnaw on the side of a bookcase.

Malg stared in disbelief. "A rabbit?" He laughed, and held his hand forward to finish his work.

Amber tried to run but fell forward, tripping over a loose cobblestone. Malg's spell, a swirling green choking gas, missed entirely, dissipating as it hit a wooden side door. Amber held his staff at Malg from the ground, trying to spin together some incantation on the drunken loom of his mind.

Before he could prepare another spell, Malg stopped and spun around, reaching for something on his back. He frantically scratched and grabbed, clawing to pull his cloak from his shoulders to relieve the itch. As he threw the cloth down, exposing his thin, grey hair and demon-possessed eyes, thousands of lady bugs crawled out from his sleeves, the neck of his robes, and every possible exit point in Malg's cumbersome clothing. The seemingly endless stream of insects took flight, creating a buzzing cloud that filled the chamber. The rabbit, upon seeing the swarm, began another frantic dash around the room, this time knocking the poor, frozen elder over, cracking his icy prison.

"ENOUGH!" Malg's voice changed, darkened, as the demon inside of him took control of his body. His eyes flared with an evil fire, and their air in the room grew acrid and hot, so tight and awful that Amber struggled to breathe. "I grow tired of these games. I will do with you what I do with pests," Malg said as he scorched the pack of ladybugs with a dash of fire.

Amber stayed on his knees, panting and coughing in the choking air. Malg drew close, unsure what to make of the old wizards actions, thinking he was setting up some elaborate trap. He lifted Amber into the air and held him there, arms out wide, unable to defend himself. Malg sneered, and whispered some indecipherable, forbidden script.

Amber woke up, soaking wet, stinking of gin. Ol'rean held out his right arm to help him up, as his left was bandaged and in a make-shift sling. Two elders were debating the best way to pull a third out of cage of iron barbs, and another was on the far side of the room, trying to calm the oversized bunny.

"None of us are quite sure what you did, Amber, but we all owe you our lives. Deema says you stopped Malg by yourself."

Deema nodded, smiled, and then winced as a healer pulled small pieces of jagged crystal from her leg.

Ol'rean pointed to the far side of the room, to an oversized keg. "There's been a lot of yelling and beating coming from the inside of that thing, but none of us even see a seam on it to open it. Not that we'd want to open it anyway, given the temperament of its current owner."

A fuzzy memory snuck back into Amber head: the last spell he'd thought of as he floated, about to die. He turned to the magister.

"I...I think that's my oak-aged stout. It's supposed to age for thirty years. I hexed it to prevent myself from sneaking any early sips."

Ol'rean laughed. "Somehow, that seems fitting. Fight fire with fire, or in this case, fire with liquid fire. I guess we had been going about your teaching the wrong way, Amber. We all owe you a debt. Perhaps it's time to reevaluate the Academy's Code." The magister walked over to Deema, moving slowly to not jostle his injury. He stood there for a moment, discussing something quietly with the other recovering elders.

"Here," the magister said, "I think these belong to you." Amber turned around to a group of smiling faces, and a hat, a sash, and a cover-robe draped over Ol'rean's arm.

But instead of the brown he expected, he saw blue.

3. ONE FOGGY THIEVING
by Jake Teeny

Alone, stumbling through the industrial block of my city, the evening sky a clammy violet, I contemplate all I own in the world: someone's discarded cigarette, my chewed up, woolen suit, and a godforsaken singing frog.

May that mongrel find his way into a middle school science classroom one day.

It wasn't always like this, just so you know. I was a respectable man once. Well, maybe not respectable, but promising. I was a promising man with a proper job and an optimistic life. People even used to compliment me on the grooming of my moustache. It was my father who said attention to detail was what made a man. Unfortunately, he never mentioned that an amphibian with a penchant for show tunes could undo all of that.

I used to work construction, or rather, deconstruction, as I cleverly called it. No greater pleasure exists than swinging a wrecking ball, that fist of God, into what other men spent so long devising. One push of a lever—whoom!—years of foresight and sweat transmogrified to dust. Still, having attended a rather prestigious (albeit less well known) university for a degree in art history, deconstruction wasn't my anticipated occupation. But all the greats have humble beginnings. Men of true promise needn't seek opportunity; opportunity seeks them. As it did for me on that foggy Friday eve.

With the city's surge for urbanization, a new structure of commerce (one of stock market dealings) was to be erected where an old office building towered. My job: to help remove the latter to allow for the former. Most of my fellow coworkers snuck off early that evening, but I, a promising man, worked as my schedule requested. For having discovered a hollowed cornerstone of that retired building, curiosity demanded I know its contents. Work with a crowbar soon detached the top of the block, wherein I found a small, mahogany box the length of my forearm. Immediately, I knew I had discovered fortune! After ensuring no one spied upon me, I blew off the dust, undid the clasp, and opened the sleek box.

You can imagine my disappointment at first seeing nothing more than a mishmash of parchment inscribed with the building's foundational date. However, as I scanned the pages (meaningless pomp about the construction of the edifice), an odd noise came from inside the box.

Ribbet.

Astonishingly—for I double-checked the letter, and that concrete block had been sealed for over sixty years—a frog hopped out. Puzzled, of course, I gawked at the animal, but other than its illogical longevity, it exhibited no unique characteristics. It was of moderate proportions, maybe a little larger than average, with dull, green skin and those misfit, bulbous eyes. It was bumpy and slimy and had that general look of apathy inherent to all of its kind.

Briefly, I entertained possible scientific rationale to explain the creature's presence (maybe an egg had incubated inside of there; maybe it had burrowed through an unseen hole), but before I could produce a reasonable conclusion, the frog—or as hindsight would reveal, the demon—behaved in a manner only attributable to forces greater than man's comprehension.

With its two front feet, it reached into the box, retrieved a miniature black top hat and cane, raised itself into a bipedal stance, and began to dance and sing. Not sing, mind you, as do frogs in their typical, guttural trumpeting, but sing, I tell you, in the voice and language of a Broadway man auditioning for a lead role.

Incredulity, accompanied by a remote sense of fear, held me, and I was at first convinced the sound came from someone singing along the sidewalk. But as I stared at that rather animated and flamboyant creature, shuffling and dancing, swinging his cane, I became certain that the noise, the music, originated inside of him. With that causal link determined, however, my next logical assessment assured my insanity.

My great Aunt Willa, a quiet woman too fond of black tea, was institutionalized for believing her spoon was a radio antenna to the Martians. Thus, sharing her bloodline, I concluded that this animal—an animal not typically proficient with English—must have been the result of my descent into delirium. Still, as I stood there reciting my name, my occupation, the square root of 144, I could not shake the distinct perception that the creature was real. We've all had dreams; we've all felt when something was merely an imaginative projection.

And I tell you with almost unwilled certitude: that frog could sing and dance.

Concluding his number (a rather gaudy song in my opinion), he flopped back into a more expectant posture and reassumed a disinterested gaze, his top hat crooked on his head like a child playing dress up with her doll. It wasn't long into his silence that dollar signs emblazoned my thoughts. The big title boards with flashing lights. Newspaper headlines. Magazine covers. I would be famous! There wouldn't be a man, woman, or child in the entire country who wouldn't know me by name.

So with my eyes gleaming from all those future paparazzi lights, I slid the frog back into its box, tucked it all beneath my jacket, and scurried home without even punching my timecard.

Back in my apartment, a modest studio I would have cleaned more frequently had I more frequent company, I sealed all my windows and doors before once more removing the animal from his containment. Although I momentarily feared the frog would not again burst into ballad (for hallucinations teem with volatility), the slimy creature, upon my opening of his cage, leapt out and into song with even more gusto than before. How stupendous, stupendous, stupendous! I thought. For as promising as my horoscope always portrayed me, not even this—this fortune, this fame—was likely bottled in its forecast.

Cleaning half a stack of dishes, unwrinkling my furrowed bed, I let my newfound friend serenade me with the sound of riffling dollar bills and standing ovations. Of course, I realized I should let another person confirm the existence of this inexplicable phenomenon, but reality has a certain weight, a definitive familiarity we are all accustomed to, and should I present this frog—this living, breathing, dancing frog—to someone else, I knew they would revel in equal

16

marvel. Instead, the notion of showing him to others stirred concern in me: men, such lustful and rapacious creatures, would likely be keen to claim this miracle for themselves. Not a coworker of mine, those bearded and crass fellows, could I trust. My friends, even those not ringing now and then to borrow money, had no particular fidelity to me. Should I showcase my discovery to any of them, I might as well cede my fortune before ever greasing a fingerprint upon it. No, I needed someone more legally bounded. Someone in the business of promoting fame without stealing it for himself. What I needed, I deduced, was a talent agency.

The ACME company had a hand in everything those days, making them not only a reputable establishment, but also a convenient one, their theatrical agency only three blocks away. So on the following morning, my best navy suit and packer hat donned, I strolled there with my boxed frog in tow.

The man I was to meet with, Mr. Buttles, was an agent of unparalleled acclaim—or so his secretary said—yet around me in the waiting room sat only bumpkins: a woman in a secondhand gown and fake mink's fur; a man in a trench coat and cowboy hat, his mustache (if I'm being frank) an insult to facial hair everywhere. And to think these individuals had proffered the same down payment to meet with Mr. Buttles. For me, the money was simply a sound investment; to them, however, it might as well have been wasted kindling.

When my name was called, I found Mr. Buttles' office a little less elegant than I had anticipated. But upon noting the seriousness of his brow and the extravagance of his bowtie, I was elated to be in such capable hands. I will admit, the fervency of my excitement prodded me into an exaggerated display—dancing and singing as my frog was about to do—but once he beheld my wonder, he, too, would join me in song and jig. Delicately, then, I opened the box and set my award-winning amphibian on his desk, placing the satin hat atop his head.

But most curiously, as I and Mr. Buttles stared at the frog, nothing happened. There was no singing. There was no dancing. The lame animal plainly sat there as though he was hearing a story for a second time and had lost all interest in the tale. Presuming stage fright, I gingerly picked up his legs and puppeteered him as he himself, unaided, had done the prior night. Alas, though, he remained limp and uncooperative, at which point I laughed nervously, replaced him in his box, and reenacted the song and dance I had promised my frog would do.

Unsurprisingly, Mr. Buttles was not impressed.

With frustration heating my neck (I had spent half my rent check to see the man!), I stormed into the hallway, only to have my frog, which in my haste to exit I had forgotten, thrown out the door after me. And then—oh, the glory! oh, the relief!—that frog, that olive green, slimy animal, hopped from his box and once more enacted a catchy tune.

Unpermitted, I rounded back into Mr. Buttles' office, enunciated and gesticulated my frog's talent, and nearly dragged the man over his desk and back into the hallway to witness it.

As I flung open the door, however, there was the frog, that cursed, irreverent frog, sitting as most frogs do: motionless and aloof, the irony of his well-timed croak lost on Mr. Buttles. For moments later, two rather burly (and I'm certain incompetent) men shoved me out the office and into the irritating brightness of the day.

Good riddance, I thought. If Mr. Buttles didn't have the patience to hear my frog sing, then he wasn't entitled to profit from his success. And as I stood on the barren sidewalk, my reptilian friend once more inspired to performance, yet another opportunity presented itself: across the street was a foreclosed theater for lease, at which point I realized, what would Mr. Buttles have done besides get me the stage I could obtain myself?

It took me most of that month to gather the funds I needed. A cash advance from work. A loan from the bank. My rainy day savings kept in a sock beneath my mattress. But with the money I needed and the vacation days from work claimed, I rented, renovated, and readied that theater for all the glory my singing frog deserved. Let Mr. Buttles choke on that!

The premiere for my show coincided with a beautiful day (a most auspicious omen), and as I stood in the back of that theater, my borrowed tuxedo crisp, the signs made, I watched my frog, umbrella in hand, dance and sing atop a tightrope strung above the stage. He was the one to show me such a feat was within his repertoire, and the exuberance I had felt upon learning this nearly drove me to kiss him—were it not for the fear he might turn into a prince.

With the spotlight prepared and the curtain drawn, I opened the door to the public, luring away their skepticism with free beer. And with over half of the small theater's seats filled, I scuttled backstage, my frog still dancing upon the wire, and pulled the rope to part the curtains. But as I hadn't replaced everything in the theater, that antiquated cord, frayed and weakened from age, snapped about three-quarters up its length. Dismayed but not discouraged (I could already imagine the collective gasp at the revelation of my prodigy), I scurried up the stairs that led to the catwalk along the ceiling. However, the broken rope, at the edge of my fingertips, would never pull back the curtains from my current position. And while I will admit that my next decision was not of sanest forethought, I jumped from the platform, clung to the rope, and let the counterweight gently lower me to the ground as the curtains opened—

—and my frog, my pea-brained, intractable frog, just sat peaceably upon the stage.

Doing nothing.

I soon forgot that my hold of the rope stayed the curtains, and upon releasing it, that hefty, maroon cloth crashed down upon me. And as the audience had apparently consumed all the beer I'd provided, a torrent of fruit took aim at my head. Although not my worst encounter with produce, obviously it was not quite the reaction I had anticipated.

The proceeding days then plundered what little stake in life I had left. The bank wanted its money. My landlord wanted his check. And before I knew it, I was shivering out a winter night on a park bench, homeless, hungry, and listening to that blasted frog wail out some new opera piece he had concocted.

Before then, I would have never guessed the Devil had such a splendid singing voice.

By this time, I of course had revisited the possibility that every number the frog performed was a manifestation of Aunt Willa's genes: the coincidence, the timing—just as someone else was about to witness the miracle—was rather suggestive. But it wasn't as though the frog didn't exist at all. People clearly saw him when presented. And we all get bashful sometimes, our best performances never to leave the mirrors of our bedrooms. This was a singing frog! An animal that transcended the scriptures of science! You're telling me, after time and time again of hearing him sing, watching him pick up that cane and kick up his legs, that you would have been willing to credit it all to fantasy? Hogwash. Though, I suppose it comes as no surprise (and may even further attenuate my credibility) that when a constable confused my frog's singing for my own in that park, no amount of babbling convinced him the amphibian was to blame.

To the psychiatric hospital we went.

In all honesty, it wasn't terrible there. They had food for me. New clothes. They even wanted me to keep my frog—enough exposure to him was bound to dispel my fanciful, anthropomorphic delusions. Of course, alone in my padded cage, the frog found no better occasion to exhibit his talents, and every time upon my release, I would ask them, Don't you hear him? Don't you hear him singing, too? And when they first admitted they did, my profundity of relief nearly elicited tears. But they quickly clarified: they heard singing, yes, but it wasn't the frog doing so; it was me. Oh, what vicious hatred for them came next! Didn't they think I'd know if I was singing? Didn't they think I'd know when I moved my own tongue, bellowed air from my own lungs? Did they think me so disconnected from my conscious processing that I couldn't even determine when I acted versus something else?

Take a few more pills, they said. Get a little more sleep.

Still of marginal sanity, I learned that no one in this facility could help me, and upon feigning complete "recovery," they released me back onto the streets from which I came. And it was at this point you found me, walking aimlessly through the industrial block of my city, the frog capped inside his box for the longest time since I had found him.

His singing. That infernal singing! Imagine, if you will, a scenario in which you know the secrets to the universe but are unable to communicate any of them. For this is how I feel. Toothpicks between my ribcage. Fleas inside my brain. A thousand different ways I've considered murdering this frog, all of which conclude with me cheerily devouring his every last appendage.

But alas, no matter how much the animal maddens me, he is a marvel…Yes, as much as I despise every molecule of his composition, he cannot be denied to this world: an artifact, maybe, of an era filled with fantastical creatures and unaccountable magic. Though maybe such compassion comes only from my newfound hope. A solution. For moments after telling you my hapless tale, I have discovered a new building in construction, its frame half complete. Yes. How perfect?! A chance to connect the ends of my circular misfortune. So with the box tight beneath my arm, I scurry inside and behold another cornerstone, hollowed as was the last.

Once more, I peek at my dumb jewel, and at the strike of light, his eyes enliven as he begins to reach for his accessories. But before a single note breaks his slimy lips, I slap the lid back down and toss him in the cornerstone.

Freedom—oh, sweet and silent liberty! I did not believe I'd have the courage, but now, rid of that hellion, no influence could make me take him back. Nearby is paper to a leave a note for the future wretch who finds him. But being as I wouldn't know the man, I feel no obligation (as the one before had felt for me) and simply clap my hands, click my heels, and zip away.

Although you may name me foolish to have discarded such a certain ticket to eminence, even the greatest glory that frog could've brought would have been less than I deserved. Therefore, my friend, if you so desire, go ahead and claim that creature for your own. I, however, have bigger, grander plans. Of course, if you do manage to cajole that frog to public display, I will expect a modest percentage of the profits for my unique effort in discovering him. Until then, though, it's back to Mr. Buttles to convince him I'm the man of promise I've always been. But first, I will need to procure myself a top hat and a cane.

4. THE BLIND WOMAN AND HER SPIDERS
by Christina Marie Keller

In a hut by the sea lived a blind woman. She was neither old nor young, but she had long white hair and was known to give the children cookies as she walked through town. Her talent in weaving was well known. Everyone had one of her famed shawls, sweaters, or rugs in their home, and most marveled that a woman struck blind could create such beautiful things. They were full of vibrant colors and made of the softest material. No one knew how she did it without seeing the yarn. The town people thought she must be magical.

The woman was magical, but not the way everyone thought. She had a secret she never told anyone: she spoke to spiders. Like her, the spiders were weavers, and the blind woman would leave them crumbs from her cookies. Out of gratitude, the spiders helped her by crawling onto her shoulder and whispering in her ear. They would tell her what yarn to use and how to weave the most intricate patterns.

One day there came distressing news from the nearby town. A warlord had arrived and demanded the people obey him. He stole their gold and silver and burned their huts to the ground. He was on his way to the blind woman's village next. The people were scared, and some fled to the nearby jungle, but others wanted to stay and fight. They did not fear the warlord and didn't want to give up their homes. When the warlord and his men marched into town, they set up camp in the town square and declared that all who wished to live should bring their gold and silver to him and the warlord would spare his or her life.

The blind woman came forward and said that she had no gold or silver. She was a poor woman who lived in a hut, and her food and little possessions were bartered from the goods she weaved. At this revelation, the warlord took no pity and said if she did not pay, she would have to work off her payment as a slave.

The blind woman cried, "Surely there is something I can give as payment? I am old, and I won't survive slavery."

The warlord thought for a moment, and then he said, "You are a weaver, so I want you to weave me a garment in a color I have never seen. If you can do this, I will consider your debt paid, and you will not be sold as a slave."

The blind woman thanked the warlord and hurried back to her hut. Once home, she combed through all of her yarn, but realized she didn't have anything new. How could she find the right color? Scared, she cried out to the spiders to help her. They came to her and soothed her fear, whispering that they would make something to save her. They would weave her a shawl out of their own webbing, and this would be her salvation. The blind woman thanked the spiders and let them do their work. All through the night the spiders worked, and by morning, they finished a shawl.

The blind woman carried the delicate webbed shawl back to the warlord. She held it out for him and hoped this garment would appease him, but the warlord shunned her gift and said that she had tricked him. She wasn't holding anything.

"No, no, I assure you. I am holding your shawl," she said. "Please, just reach out and touch it."

He reached out his hand and to his astonishment, he felt the webbing. Backing away, he could not believe his eyes. There was nothing in her hand, but he felt the fabric. "Witch," he cried. "You used sorcery to make this!"

The blind woman said nothing and continued to hold the shawl in front of her. She didn't know what to do. Would he sell her into slavery for being a witch?

On and on the warlord cried about sorcery, until he convinced himself that the whole town housed witches like her, and he fled as fast as he horse would carry him.

The town rejoiced and called the blind woman their savior. They knew that even if she was a witch, she was a kind woman who had saved their homes and kept them from slavery. For weeks they brought gifts and treats of thanks to her door. She accepted the gifts and promised everyone a new coat for winter. But she always left crumbs for the spiders, because they were the true saviors.

5. AYE, 'TWAS ME
By Tara Campbell

Aye, 'twas me what laid him low, and I don't feel a whit o regret fer it.

'Twas him what started it all, takin' up with that hussy ginger up-village, leavin' me weepin' and pinin', cryin' fer fergiveness he weren't fit to give. Fer it weren't no failin' on my part led him 'tween the thighs o that frowzy harlot; that graspin', stinkin' fleshpot. 'Twas his own base instinct, and the only shame I carry is havin' ever loved him at all.

I sat alone too long, I did, cryin' me eyes out fer that rat of a man. Couldn't take seein' 'em together, burned with grief and shame to come upon 'em in the lane, smilin' and makin' eyes like cow-brained fools. *May they both burn*, I'd say to meself—most un-Christian, but I couldn't help it. Couldn't think about nothin' else when I saw 'em in the square. So I stopped goin' out. Didn't leave me house. Couldn't stand to see their faces beamin' with a bliss I used to know; couldn't bear to breathe in the odor o sex and sin they trailed behind 'em.

Aye, I sat, and I hurt. Ruined, I was. No one else would want me now, and I didn't want no one but him.

I sat, and I hurt, and I didn't eat. Friends stopped in, then stopped altogether—I weren't much fer company. I sat, and hurt, and didn't eat and didn't speak a word to nobody, not even to meself. Just stopped bein'. Shrank down, small and hard, until I weren't meself no more; 'til one mornin' I woke up, and I really weren't even a woman no more.

'Twas like the Princess and the Pea that mornin', only I weren't no princess. Aye, and so I was the pea—at least the size and shape o one. Right flummoxed I was; didn't know what to do but roll on out o bed. Roll I did, and hit the floor with a *clack* and kept on rollin' o'er the floorboards. Was right worried I wouldn't be able to open the door, but really 'twas no need: I rolled right underneath it out into the lane.

Well, I rolled into the village, wailin' and hollerin' fer help. But o course no one had a whit o sense. Couldn't figure out there was a bloomin' pea jumpin' and rollin' o'er the cobbles, screamin' fer all she was worth. Bunch o blind mice, them people. But the cats—oh the cats, now they had a bleedin' field day, pouncin' and scratchin' after me. Well, I weren't no fool; settled right into a granary and kept me distance, kept real quiet 'til I could have a good think.

As I's waitin' fer me brain to think up a plan, I tried to get a better look at meself. Weren't much to see: didn't have no arms nor legs no more, and no matter which direction I looked, all I could see's a kind o dark curve, like I's lookin' over a ball. Only now that ball was me. Seems I's quite right to be settin' up with the grain in me new condition, but what kind of grain I might be, I'd no bloody idea. I weren't hops nor barley nor wheat nor nothin' I'd ever seen before. And I weren't no stone, I didn't think, cause no piece o rock could ever feel so afraid as I did.

Well, then came a plan. If this was the granary, I thought, better to get back into a kitchen than to risk goin' back out into the lane. Jumpin' around in some baker's bowl'd be better than pleadin' me case in the gutter to a rat. So I wriggled meself up the pile o grain—wheat it turned out to be—and rolled right up to a crack o light I figgered come from the door. Buried meself in a little fer good measure, lest they take me fer a pebble and toss me out on me ear—if I still had one.

Well, weren't too long before I heard a *creak* and a *bang* and the granary filled up with light, it did. Saw it through the layer o wheat atop me, and I started prayin' to wind up in the kitchen o some kindly woman with a heart as soft as the butter meltin' on her counter. Weren't thinkin' too straight, though. Weren't thinkin' about all what has to happen between wheat and flour.

I tell you, I never had such a whoopin', threshin' and floggin' in me life. Wheat from chaff is all I can say 'bout that. Wheat from chaff, and there me in the mix too. And then come the grindin', and it was all I could do to jump and hop and hope fer a miracle; kinda figgered I was due one by then. Then the whole kit and caboodle shifted and slid and finally came to rest in what I'm guessin' was a barrel, cause then things got real dark and quiet.

Well, I sat and I prayed, and I finally got me miracle. After bein' moved and shook and shifted and sifted, I finally heard voices again. And who d'you think I'd be hearin' but him, the very man what made me sink so low and shrink so small, askin' after a bit o flour. Hearin' his deep, wonderful voice was all I needed to start buildin' up a little bit o hope, 'spite everything. He'd recognize me; surely I could talk him into helpin' me. I wriggled meself up, high enough to get picked up but still deep enough to stay hid; and wouldn't you know it, salvation came in the form of a scoop and a bag.

All the way home, bumpin' along with his veggies and grains, I started wonderin' how it come that he's doin' the shoppin' himself. Started to think he'd left the ginger harlot and was livin' on his own again, havin' to cook fer himself, me not bein' available or even known to anyone in me current form. Poor little lamb, I thought, poor little chook, havin' to make like he knows what goes on in a kitchen. Must be too distraught to head to a pub, likely in mournin', havin' thought he lost me ferever. Won't that just be somethin', I said to meself, when he pours me out and finds me again.

Well, the noise o the town centre quieted down, and I heard a door open and shut. Then I figgered we was home, 'cause he set his things down. But soon's we stopped movin', the groceries and me, me dreams was dashed, cause I heard it. There was I, fixin' to wrestle me way up to the top o the sack, to make meself heard and get meself back into me sweetie's hand and heart—until I heard that woman's voice. That weasel what took me man. I heard that wheedlin' prattle tumblin' out o that slobberin' cow, that mongrel what took me should've-been husband, and I lay quite still. Knew right then things weren't gonna work out that good fer nobody.

Well, I tell you, what torture, havin' to hear 'em croon and swoon over the evenin' meal. I sat and stewed all night, not wantin' to imagine what they got up to after they left the kitchen. I was right sick, I was, and would o thrown up had I still got a gullet.

And soon's he went off to work the next mornin', she launched into the kitchen again, greedy little sow, gobblin' up all his hard-earned wages. Slurpin' and chewin' and rippin' into grocery packets like a starvin' whelp. Well soon enough she ripped into me packet and started measurin' out cupfuls o flour fer bread. *Aye, bake me in*, I thought. *Bake me in and I'll hack meself out o you.*

And then I was in another dance again, gettin' scooped up, mixed in, kneaded, punched and pounded. Tryin' to pull meself around in the dough to keep from gettin' picked out. Sure and she felt me in there, but I could always move around just enough to stay away from her graspin' claws. She finally gave up, I suppose, and just plopped me in the pan with the rest of it. Figgered she'd find me when she cut in to the loaf, mayhaps. But then, oh the heat! She shut me up in that oven and I baked and ached in heat you couldn't imagine. Couldn't roll nowhere else, stuck in a roastin' inferno. Wondered if I'd be alive to know me own revenge. But me anger was hotter'n than any oven. I burned happily just knowin' I still had a chance to cause her pain.

After what seemed like years, the little harlot released her bread from the infernal pit, with me baked right in. I's barely conscious, but I felt everything start to cool down. 'Twas a wonder I didn't keep the whole loaf cookin' with the heat o me misery. *Come and take a slice*, said I under me breath (like I still had lungs to breathe), *and I'll show you what true love feels like.*

"Well, that ravenous beast started tearin' into the loaf before it was even cooled all the way, sawin' away thick, steamin' slabs and stuffin' 'em down her gullet. All I could do was wait 'till she got to me. She hacked off another slice and light flooded into me loaf. I's next.

Then I heard me dear sweet's voice ring out—he was back from work, he was—and her gratin' squawk in return. She took a knife to the loaf again and cut off a hunk—with me finally in it! Light was shinin' in from both sides now, and I felt me slice heavin' through the air.

Then the great ugly she-pigeon squawked again.

"Here, me sweet," said she. "After a long, hard day o work, you surely need a little bit o bread."

"No, me love," said he, "You have it. You need your strength fer the little mite growin' inside you. *Our* little mite."

If bread could boil, I'dve scalded that scabby she-rat's hand in a second. After all the times I tried to conceive, knowin' fer sure he'd

28

stay, here and she gets with child at the snap of a finger. I heard her inane gigglin' gettin' ever closer, which means I's gettin' ever closer to her rancid little mouth. Funny thing, the closer I come to executin' me plan, the nervouser I got. And weren't I supposed to be lookin' forward to teachin' her a little lesson in misery, the schemin' little snake, carryin' that child what should've been mine—with the man what should've been mine?

But then, thought I, there's a child in there. Sprung from fickle seed in the wrong belly, but a child nonetheless. And she, the mangy little she-devil bearin' it—aye, but who could ever blame a woman fer wantin' a child?

Well, I's thinkin' all this at the very moment I's headin' straight into that woman's gapin' maw, and I'm tellin' you, if I'da had legs I'da backpedaled like the drunk what proposed to the farmer's daughter the night before. But I didn't have no choice, did I? *In I go*, thought I, but no! Suddenly the tide turned: the little vixen laughed and steered me flyin' carpet o bread away from her quiverin' lips and popped me right into me man's still-devilishly-lovely mouth. But oh, too late, too late! Now that I had me chance to get in there and vent me anger, show him how much he turned me inside out by tearin' his insides up—I couldn't even think on it. That little babe growin' inside that woman hadn't done nobody no harm. That little babe needed a chance to live, and with both mother and father, even though they both broke me heart.

And seein' as how I didn't have no business in nobody's stomach no more, I sure as shade weren't gonna go down there. He was chewin' by this time, so I had to act quick. I wriggled around and made sure he'd bite down on me: a man could be a father even missin' a tooth. Well, he yelped and cursed—I cracked that thing right in two, I did—and he spat me out. I rolled away into a corner, where they didn't pay me no mind. I watched him moan and groan and sop up the blood and head out to the doctor.

Well, they didn't have no money fer a new tooth, so fer the rest o his days he went without. Left a big hole when he smiled—not that he smiled much anymore. Sure and I watched him change. Never realized what a vain little bastard he was till I saw him without that tooth. Got all surly and mean, thought everyone at the pub was starin' at what weren't there no more, so he started drinkin' at home. Then he complained that not goin' out made him feel like a caged beast. Started actin' like one too, grumblin' and cursin' and beatin' on his new missus, and soon enough she left with the baby. Just up and left like it weren't the end of the world to let go. I was in awe.

Well, he could o went after 'em right then and there, but instead he just sat and opened another bottle.

Aye, I thought, *he's in pain, but surely after this one he'll realize what he done and go after 'em.* But no, he opened up another bottle.

Aye, I thought again, *after this one he'll surely weep at his foolishness and go after 'em and seek their forgiveness.* But no, he opened up yet another bottle.

Day after day, I watched him open bottle after bottle; watched him keep drinkin' and fallin' further into despair. He didn't hardly stir an inch, just sat and drank and cursed and sat and drank some more, until one day he probably woke up a small, hard round nothin' like me. But that last part's just a guess, seein' as how I went on with me life without him.

I'd had enough o that life, enough o self pity and darkness. I up and rolled away, I did, watchin' and listenin', tryin' to find out where that mother and babe had got to. Miles covered, people met, chances taken, all another tale fer another time. But find 'em I did. I rolled over to their cottage and planted meself right by that little babe's window. I prayed and prayed, announced me intention you might say, until finally I sprouted. My skin split, and a shoot come up out o me, reachin' into the sky above; roots dug down into the dirt below. Nobody knew what I was, but everyone marveled at how quick I grew.

I kept on growin' and so did that little girl. She babbled and patted me spindly little trunk. She learned to run and I was always the finish line. When I's strong enough they tied a swing to me arm and she whirled and swayed and sang songs up into me branches. I grew even stronger and she climbed up me body and sat in me arms and told me stories and dreams fer hours and hours. And now she's of an age where lads are startin' to come 'round. One of 'em'll carve both o their initials into me side, and then she'll leave, and I won't be able to roll after her no more. And I can only hope she'll be happy with him, but I know if she's not, she won't be afraid to leave. Her mother taught her that by leavin' me lovely; and by breakin' his tooth, I's the one made him show his true colors in the first place. So the way I figger it, me and her mother, we was a team. And we raised

30

our girl right.

So aye, as I said from the start, 'twas me what laid him low, and I don't feel a whit o regret fer it.

6. THE BIG BAD WOLF IS A LIE
by Susan Bianculli

Pssst! Hey, hey you! C'mere. I can't hurt you from inside this iron barred cage. You're new around here, aren't you? You look like a kind soul, and I gotta have someone who hasn't been around before to listen to me. C'mon, it won't take long, okay? You will? Great!

You can see that I'm just a wolf, right? Okay, I'm a big black wolf, but that's beside the point—I'm still a wolf. Have you heard yet that the locals are calling me the Big Bad Wolf? Oh, you have already? Well, let me tell you, that's a lie. Mostly.

Look, I'm no more "bad" than anybody else, and definitely better than some I could name. But because certain people needed a patsy for a cover-up, and because I've been known to, uh, cull sheep from local farmers from time-to-time, which has given me something of an off reputation, I've ended up in a dog kennel with a thick collar of leather around my neck. And why is that?

I'll tell you why in four words: Little Red Riding Hood.

Heard of her? Yeah, I can see by your face that you have. Her name is more descriptive than you'd think. Most people not from around here assume that it's a red-colored cloak with a hood which gave her that nickname. And she does have one like that which she wears for special occasions. But her name isn't from it. Here, let me break it down for you. "Little"—yeah, that's her size and age. She's barely five feet tall if she stands on her tiptoes, and she's only 14. "Red" —well, that's the color of her waist length hair that she generally leaves down. Everybody calls her "Red" because of it, even though her birth name is Gwendolyn. Red is *not* the color of the cloak she usually wears; that's a good, serviceable brown cloth. I should know. "Riding"—ah, we'll come to the reason why I am where I am now because of that part of her name later in the story. And finally, "Hood"—that's her family last name, and the only part of her name that's real. She's the descendant of some English guy who ran around in another forest called Sherwood back in the Dark Ages robbing people, which for some reason was appreciated back then. Weird, isn't it?

Red and her family make a big to-do about their last name, and people in the village seem to respect them because of it. That, and the fact that Red's family is well-off because of great-something Grandpa Hood. Me, I don't understand why people's reputations aren't based on what they do, but on whatever your however-many-times-back relative did. My reputation may not be the best, but the farmers around here have never really put up too big of a stink about me. I help them out by taking care of killing the weaklings in their flocks that they don't want to deal with. It's a win-win: the farmers don't get their hands dirty, their flocks stay close to the shepherds from fear of me, and I get a free couple of meals off of each cull. If the farmers didn't want me to do it, they could have stopped me years ago. They turn a blind eye when they see me cut a cull; they just like to grumble and complain and spout off in town meetings about me to save face. Their words are just hot air, though; they've never done any of the stuff they've talked about. That's the status quo around here.

But now the status quo has been upset, all because of that stupid girl. And because people seem to respect the last name Hood more than they should. Here, let me tell you what really happened.

You see, I was headed home to my den through the woods about a week ago. It was late at night, and I was carrying half of a scrawny lamb in my mouth to put up in my larder later. Out of the corner of my eye, I saw a flash of red in the moonlight on the nearby path. I thought that was kind of weird, so I cached the lamb meat in a hollow log that happened to be nearby, marked it the way we wolves do, and headed off in the direction I'd seen the red flash. Since I wasn't sure what it was, I darted from tree to bush to fern while making towards the path—anything that would keep me out of the sight of whatever the red thing was in case it was something dangerous. The woods can be risky at night to those who aren't careful. But cats aren't the only animals who will sacrifice safety for curiosity.

Boy, was I surprised to see what it was when I caught up with it. Or rather, who it was. You guessed it; it was Little Red Riding Hood.

I popped out onto the path in front of her and said, "Hey there, Red. What brings you out so late in the woods?"

I swear she jumped nearly as high as my shoulder, and that's saying something. That should have been my first warning.

"My—my mother said I shouldn't talk to strangers!" she said.

She looked flustered, and a flash of guilt crossed her face for just a second. That should have been my second warning.

I frowned. "I'm hardly a stranger, Red. You know me well enough to say hello when we run into each other during the day. But these woods aren't really safe at night, remember? There's lots of old fairy magic that can get loose in the dark. Do you really want a run-in with a troll or something?"

She smoothed the sturdy brown fabric of her cape with her hands.

"I'm wearing my cloak inside-out. I'm not stupid," she retorted.

I rolled my eyes. "Yeah, that would handle a spell cast at you. But not troll teeth, or anything else that could touch you. Here, let me escort you to help keep you safe. Where are you going?"

"To..." she stopped, took a breath, and then said, "To Granny's house."

I shrugged. "Okay. Let's go."

Most people slept at night as far as I knew, but who was I to know about human family visiting hours? I know different now, of course.

We walked together in silence through the wooded path, following its different forkings to Granny's. I noted to myself each person who lived down each of the other paths we passed: the three little Pigs down this one, Hansel and Gretel down that one, any number of wood choppers down others—I can go on and on, if you want. I know everybody out in the woods, and they know me. We forest folk have a sort of live-and-let live approach to each other, and it works out just fine. Or at least, it did.

Anyway, as we walked I could see something was wrong with Red because she kept twisting the right edge of her inside out cloak with nervous fingers. I put it down to her being reminded of what could be out here in the woods, and dismissed it from my mind.

When we were near the last fork in the path which would lead to Granny's, she said, "Hey, Wolfie, thanks for the escort, but I can make it from here. Granny's is just up ahead on the left, you know."

I winced a little at the overly familiar nickname. "It's not far now, Red. I can take you all the way to Granny's door."

"No, really, it's fine. I'll be fine. Everything's fine and I'm sure you want to get to your den or wherever it is you were going before you went out of your way for me," she insisted with what I now know was an unnatural cheerfulness.

Now, I've never been one to force myself on anyone who didn't want me to be around. So with reluctance I said, "Okay, Red, if you're sure you don't want me to walk you all the way."

I turned around and left her there, intending to head straight back to the hollow log and pick up my dinner for the next two days. I curse the fact that I happened to look back over my shoulder at her when the path was almost out of sight for me. That let me see that she was walking on the right fork, not the left.

Fearing that she'd somehow been put under a fairy spell despite her inside out cloak, I dashed back towards her. I didn't yell at her to hold up, because if she'd been under a spell she wouldn't have listened anyway, and it would have only alerted whatever held her. I reached the fork and saw her disappearing out of sight around the next curve in the path. She had to have been moving pretty fast after we parted to get that far. I put on a burst of speed to catch up to her, but did a four-paw skid to a stop at the sight I saw as I rounded the same curve she'd had.

There was a reason she'd taken the right fork after all, and it wasn't fairy magic. There on the path I saw Red in the arms of the wood chopper's teenaged apprentice. Well, no, not just in the arms of, but she had jumped up and wrapped her legs around his waist as well.

And that's where the "Riding" part of her name comes from. She used to jump up on villagers and demand piggy back rides from them when she was littler, but as she grew up it mostly stopped, except for her doing it with one particular guy. Everybody knows that around here. But what everybody doesn't know is that this boy Hoban wasn't the guy she should have been "riding" like that. The guy she was *supposed* to be doing that with is named Jeralan, who is the assistant baker in the village. Even though I'm a wolf, I know humans tend to frown on people kissing like they were doing when one of them is supposed to be with someone else.

Well, Red and Hoban were kissing for all they were worth—right out in the open in the fairy-magic-tainted woods late at night in the moonlight. And you do know that that's a recipe for disaster, don't you? I could see the fairy magic was attracted to the young lovers' passion for each other. Wisps of enchantment came together behind them, fast. A form took shape from the wisps even before the magic had become solid, and was already slowly reaching out toward them. The teenagers had to have been really involved with each other for that to have happened. That was bad.

"Stop!" I shouted at the two idiots, who were somehow still oblivious to their danger.

I rushed at them to break them up, hoping that that would stop the magic from being fed enough to make whatever it was trying to make.

They broke apart, and Red jumped down to the ground. They whirled to face me, startled at my charge. Red screamed, not understanding that I was trying to save her and Hoban's lives, and ducked behind the wood cutter's apprentice. Hoban crouched down and scrabbled at the side of the path for his axe. At least he'd come armed with sharp iron into the woods, I have to give him that.

Not wanting to get a face full of axe, I skidded to a second stop just out of swing range and yelled, "You idiots! Strong emotions in the open woods at night are going to get you killed! Run for Granny's! Now!"

Red, over her scare when she realized it was only me, moved to stand next to Hoban and huffed, "You have no right to be telling me what to do! You're not my mother! Or my father!"

I growled, "And it's a good thing too, else you'd be across my knee now—if I had a human knee and a human hand to spank your bottom with! Now move!"

Hoban of course jumped to her defense. "Now see here, Wolf, you can't talk to her that way!"

He swung the axe in a repeated slow arc between them and me to keep me at bay, as if he thought I was going to try and hurt them or something.

I snarled, "Oh, yes I can talk that way, when..."

My words trailed off as I looked beyond them. My eyes widened.

I'd been too late. My charge hadn't been quick enough to stop the magic growing, and now the angry emotions that were swirling about the three of us added themselves to the passionate magical energy of before. A faceless, blobby tentacled monster appeared, rooted to the path just behind the two teenagers. It was colored in swirls of red and purple by love and anger—two of the strongest human emotions.

"Look out behind you!" I yelled, as I foolishly ran forward to knock them out of its reach despite the axe the wood cutter's apprentice still waved about.

Hoban, whom I considered the smarter of the two humans, glanced back over his shoulder at my words. What I could see of his face in the moonlight turned white. I have to give him credit again—he shoved Red with rough hands out of a tentacle's reach just before it became solid. She stumbled into the woods away from it, and screamed in a higher pitch than last time when she saw why he'd pushed her. I ducked under Hoban's weapon and barreled into him, shoving him out of reach of another monstrous limb the other way across the path.

But I wasn't so lucky. The ugly blob grabbed me with the tentacles meant for Hoban and Red and tried to lift me. It was a good thing I am a big wolf, and that it was still newly formed. It strained, but couldn't move me. All it could do was squeeze, but that was enough.

"Help!" I gasped breathlessly, struggling to get away.

A shrill voice replied, "Hoban, no! Don't help him! He may be a wolf, but he can expose us! Just let the creature have him!"

I was shocked. I couldn't believe my ears. Red was willing to let me die to protect her secret meeting with Hoban? My struggles weakened with the loss of my air.

I turned pleading eyes on the wood cutter's apprentice. One swipe with that iron axe, and the fairy magic would be disrupted.

"Please," I whispered, almost out of breath.

I heard a sickening crack, and an incredible pain shot through my left side. The monster had not just cracked, but broken, one of my ribs. Unless Hoban did something then, the others would crack one right after the other, then my spine would go, and then I'd die.

But that breaking rib saved me. Hoban jumped at the sound—it had been loud. He swung at the tentacles holding me. I wanted to howl at him to hit the body instead of them, but couldn't. My lungs were empty. Hoban sliced through the tentacles and made the creature flash into nothingness. Unfortunately, the axe's momentum meant that the blade buried itself in my side. I gasped from the pain, and died.

Well, okay, that was a little exaggeration there. I didn't die. But I did wake up in here. Somehow Hoban must have talked Red into getting me help. I'd like to thank him for that, at least, but I haven't seen either him or Red since that night. I've overheard bits and pieces of the story from passersby about how the two teenagers somehow got me to Granny's and put me in her bed so the old woman could work on sewing up the gash in my side. Granny then put some healing herb paste on her handiwork from a basket of goodies Red had brought over earlier in the week, and bandaged it in place. My ribs were bound by a separate length of cloth to hold the broken bone in place before the three of them brought me to the village.

But nobody here will talk to me directly about any of what happened. That's because while I was unconscious, Red spread this ridiculous story about me following her through the woods, going to Granny's house and pretending to be her, eating Granny, then cross-dressing and waiting to eat Red as well when she came for a visit. I was tried and sentenced for those "crimes" while I was still out cold. I can only guess it's because of the Hood name that Red was taken at her word.

Can you believe it? All you have to do is look and see that Granny is still alive! I saw her myself at a distance just the other day, with no teeth marks on her or anything! I ask you, why in the world would I go after humans when I have this sweet lamb arrangement with the farmers already? Plus I'm nowhere near starving, even if I didn't have the culling to do. And eating someone I know would just be wrong.

I can only guess that Red came up with some even more ridiculous explanation for Granny still being here during my sentencing—something like that I was so hungry that I swallowed Granny whole, and when Hoban came to rescue Red from me, he cut me open and Granny popped out unharmed. Granny must be protecting the Hood reputation, which I guess is why she's going along with this stupidness.

So, can you please spread my story? Let people know I've been framed, and that I don't deserve this? I'd appreciate it. And if you can get enough people to know the truth and I am set free, I promise I'll share the next lamb I cull with you.

I'll even let you cook it first.

Deal?

7. WHAT GOES AROUND
by Arthur M. Doweyko

By the time Doctor George Dowd finished sewing up his good friend Paul Scott's arm, the late summer sun peered over the serrated edges of the Sierra Nevada. The sounds of picks, shovels and wagons rolling outside the shack reminded him that, although it was twenty years since the strike at Sutter's Mill, the folks in Deely's Creek still managed to scrape out a living from the spent pits dotting the landscape.

"That should do it, Paul. Just keep it clean, and get some rest."

"I'm really grateful, Doc."

Paul diverted his eyes to the floor. The abrupt silence spoke volumes.

George smiled as he packed his satchel. "I'll be by in a couple of days to check up on you. Lucky I came by when I did. This ain't my usual route."

Paul walked over to a corner, brought up a small sack and undid the ties. "I don't think luck's got anything to do with it. A couple years back, I did a favor for a fellow back in town. He paid me with this."

Paul lifted out something bulky glinting white and gold.

"Turns out he was a Shoshone medicine man. Said it was guaranteed to bring the owner good luck."

Paul raised it up for Dowd to see.

"And he was right. If you hadn't come by when you did, I'd likely be crippled or worse. You and this arm—that was more than coincidence. It was *this*."

George looked at the miniature stage coach Paul held up. It was made of hand-carved wood and finely detailed in glossy paint. He could almost see tiny people stepping onto the coach's steps, dressed up in finery, men holding the doors open while tipping their hats to the women passengers. Then he caught on.

"You say a Shoshone gave you this?"

"The man said he just happened to come across a broken down wagon over them mountains … in the desert. If he hadn't, it's likely the passengers would have died. It was a gift from a little boy. A way of sayin' thanks."

"I can't take that."

"You ain't got no choice. I *have* to give it to you. The favor needs to pass on."

"It's way too much. It'd make a fine gift for someone special, but not for me."

Paul shook his head and stood his ground. "You don't get it. You have to take it." Paul tilted his head to a side and added, "You've got a boy, right? This here's a present for him."

The workmanship was spectacular. Gold trim ran along the windows and the corners of the carriage. The wheels, especially, glowed with a life of their own. The master craftsman who created the model had an eye for detail. To his five year old son, Archie, bedridden for most of his short life, playthings were a blessed diversion.

George shrugged and nodded. "All right, Paul. You just take care of that arm."

"You watch and see. It'll bring you good luck just like it did for me."

At midnight a lone wagon wheel rolled into town. The white rim, embraced by a painted gold metal strip, tapped out a mournful soliloquy on the rocky surface of Main Street. It paused at a corner as if to check the street name. Impossibly balanced, it rotated in place a full quarter turn, and resumed its travel, heading directly toward Johnson's Livery.

Werner Johnson awoke with a start. A gentle morning breeze pushed aside the yellowed lace curtain of his second floor bedroom window.

He swung out of bed and ran a hand over his chin.

"You up yet, Wern?"

It was his wife in the kitchen downstairs.

"Yeah, yeah."

He could smell the pancakes and the coffee. "I'll be right there." A rumble erupted from his stomach.

He was sitting at the table gobbling pancakes when his wife asked, "You ain't washed up, are you?" His mouth was full as he mumbled something incomprehensible. He sucked up a slug of black gruel, slipped out the back door to the livery, and yelled back. "Ain't got no time. It's past eight, and Mack'll be lookin' for his wagon."

Denton Mackenzie was the owner of the general store and the richest man in Deely's Creek. The morning train carried mining supplies, and Mackenzie needed the wagon. It was a heavy blue Murphy model, the kind with wheels taller than most men. One of those wheels needed mending, and Werner had promised it'd be ready this morning.

He cursed as he shuffled across the corral to where the wagon stood propped up on a set of clay bricks. The broken wheel lay by the protruding skein—beyond repair. He hoisted it up and rolled it to the junk pile. When he saw another wheel leaning on the railing a few yards off, his jaw dropped. It was whole and intact, though from where he stood, it looked a bit too small for the Murphy.

"How in blazes?"

As he approached, he looked around and then back at it again, afraid that the wheel might be an apparition of sorts, maybe a mirage about to wink out and turn into the sun-bleached dirt beneath it.

But it stayed put, and now looked a might larger. Werner canted it up and rolled it to the waiting wagon. White flecks of paint clung to its finely turned spokes. He used both arms to position the wheel box up against the skein.

"Well, I'll be. It's a perfect fit."

"Are ya gonna put it on, or just stand there admirin' it?" Denton Mackenzie lifted the brim of his Stetson. "Have any trouble fixin' it?"

Werner was about to explain that it was a different wheel when he noticed that the white paint was gone, leaving behind deep blue spokes and rim—a perfect match for Mackenzie's wagon. Maybe he wasn't quite awake yet.

"No, no problem."

"I'm gonna need the wagon straightaway. A delivery's comin' in on the early train, so maybe you can speed it up some?"

It was mid-morning when George Dowd stepped out of Deely's Central Bank. His son sat on a bench in front of Ferguson's Barber Shop. Archie was hunched over his toy wagon. It was the other reason they had come into town. A wheel had loosened and fallen off. They searched the house from top to bottom and came up empty-handed. Their next stop was the Wanamaker's Toy Shop just down the street.

George paused at the edge of the wooden walkway and waved to Archie. Morning traffic was light—a couple of horses, a few pedestrians, and far off, men unloading a wagon. Archie hoisted himself up with his crutch.

At that moment George heard a shout followed by another. He was half-way across when he turned toward the commotion. People on foot and riders were streaming left and right, opening a path for a large blue wagon. Four horses strained at their reins, pulling the driverless wagon, sending crates and sacks into the street.

George's mind raced and time slowed to a flip book version of events, each page carrying the next scene. He saw Archie clambering off the curb, crutch beneath one shoulder, his face ringed by a broad smile. The four black stallions, their eyes wild and mouths quivering, heaved forward. Behind them, a magnificent cobalt blue wagon loomed into view. People stumbled and fell in every direction.

His legs dragged, as if in mud. He took a step toward Archie. The oncoming juggernaut swept people aside. Nearby, an elderly woman collapsed on the walkway.

Archie, his crutch gone, was now in the street. The teetering maelstrom was upon them. George lunged and fell upon his son, shielding Archie's frail body, and braced himself for the deadly crush of hooves and wheels.

He heard a loud crack and raised his head in time to see the wagon swerve, twist and flip on its side. The horses broke free and split into pairs, galloping inches past the two prostrate figures, covering them in dust. The wagon toppled and gouged an arc in the baked earth, spilling the rest of its load. George lifted his head in time to see a barrel roll to a stop at his son's feet.

"Archie, are you all right?"

Archie sputtered, spitting out dirt. It was a joyous sound.

The first to reach the pair was Werner Johnson. "You okay? Damn. One of the wheels plumb flew off. You and your son are awful lucky."

George nodded, still in a daze.

"Dad, dad, look at this." Archie picked up his wagon from the street.

George braced himself for the wreck that the little stagecoach must have become. "That's okay, son. We came into town to get that thing fixed, and that's what we'll do."

When his son brought up the model, George nearly collapsed.

"I'll be damned. It survived, and that missing wheel ... it's back?"

Maybe it was the play of light on the toy. At first, the wheel looked blue, but as Archie swung it up from shadow to light, the fine filigreed white and gold gleamed back. George squeezed his eyes shut and looked again. His breath caught. He was speechless.

The buckboard ride home was quiet. His son sat in the seat next to him, gliding the toy stagecoach across his lap as if it was trundling across mountain valleys. Once in a while, their eyes met. George wiped his eyes and snapped the reins.

Well paid, Paul, well paid.

8. LOOKING FOR GODS
by Stefen Styrsky

As Matthew hurried down the ferry's gangplank, Professor Haft's words returned to him: "Just don't go looking for gods."

The sun had nearly set, and he was eager to find a place to stay before dark. The journey from Karpathos had taken longer than expected. Already the quayside buildings were in shadow, though enough light remained that the black water along the docks glistened with foamed, oily rings. He made the pier just as a horn blast from a fishing boat boomed back at him off faceless walls.

Professor Haft had entirely understood Matthew's thesis block. "Many people can't write when it's time," he'd said, cleaning his glasses with his shirttail. "Many people just need a break. They come back with renewed enthusiasm." Matthew had heard as much.

What Haft didn't know was that the block originated with Gregory's transfer to another school and another city—and no invitation that Matthew should follow. Matthew felt as if his student years, his life, had also departed in Gregory's suitcase. His thesis, among the least of things, packed and shipped away.

He thought what he needed was a quick fling to Greece. A way to forget about Gregory, to stop concentrating on the dark corners of his apartment. There was one trip at the end of undergraduate work, a brief whirl through Athens and Delphi, but since then, his only experience had come from books. He decided a second, less formal tour, might help.

But the gods had fled Athens. The Acropolis itself was a

disappointment. Sweating, huffing people moved in clots through the temple complex, and distant traffic noises spoiled any aura of reverence. He thought he detected the sting of tear gas, a remnant of recent activity. He felt hot and dizzy. Men, women, and children in shorts and baseball caps shuffled about and snapped photographs. People with people; the reason he had left in the first place. Athens was too close.

Consulting his Lonely Planet guidebook, he had found what was described as a sufficiently deserted island. It was only a short charter flight away on Olympia Air to Karpathos and then a ferry from there. Fortunately, the next plane left in the morning.

Of the few places the book suggested to stay in the port town, the first he came upon was a small grocery that rented rooms on its second floor. The proprietor showed him around back, where stairs led to the rooms above. He paid for a week, and at a cafe next door bought some dolmas and lamb off the spit.

Matthew ate on a bench in the town square. At the square's center posed the statue of some war hero, and light and music spilled into the area from two taverns. Tomorrow he'd find an appropriately abandoned beach and try to forget Gregory and his failed thesis.

A dozen feet away, five young men gathered around a bench in the glow of a lamp post. They talked loudly, but he couldn't understand them. Drunk, they laughed in boisterous, sharp barks and pranced around, mock boxing with each other.

One boy was quieter than the others. He sat atop the bench's back while his friends darted around him. He returned Matthew's stare without seeming intruded upon. Even from a distance, Matthew could see the boy was what was described two thousand years ago as "youth at its loveliest," making him perhaps twenty, twenty-one.

His arms were toned, not yet sinewy like the older men who had worked the ropes on the ferry; his skin dark was lustrous in that way only young skin glows. A companion offered him a cigarette. He shook his head, but took a deep swallow when the same friend proffered a small flask. The boy stood and walked off, friends following. He wore sandals, and Matthew strained to glimpse what he could of his flashing ankles and toes.

Matthew rented a motor scooter and studied a map for beaches. "Where should I go?" he asked the grocery owner.

"Here," the man said, pointing to a spot southeast on the coast. "All along here are good beaches."

"What about here?" The black line of a road bypassed a long hook of seashore that jutted into the ocean. There might be isolated coves there.

The man shook his head. "Dry. No place to get water or food. The beach is rocky."

He thanked the man and decided he'd camp on whatever beach he found to avoid going back and forth. He took provisions and several bottles of water.

The ride was over hills, which revealed the bright sea when he reached the crests. At the top of one, he glimpsed what he thought was the stretch of land the grocer had told him to avoid. Far from looking dry, trees grew among the crags in the distance. A faint dirt road branched off in the same direction, and he steered the moped onto it, descending into a maze of narrow ravines and valleys. At some point a dog lying in the dust scuttled up a hillside and out of his way and then turned a gaping jaw to watch him pass.

Around a hill the beach came into view—a white palette of fine, near-blinding sand. He braked and turned off the engine. The sand continued on for some distance, then stopped as the ground rose again. Farther up there was a dilapidated house, beyond which stood the olive trees. The grocery proprietor must have only heard what this place was like, for the beach looked perfect.

He walked the moped in the gravel and scrub along the beach's edge. The house sat in great disrepair. It leaned crazily to one side, on the verge of collapse. Wide, leprous strips of paint had weathered off the siding, and the exposed wood was warped and split. Shutters hung open before cracked windows.

In back there was a pump. The rusted handle cackled when he moved it up and down. A brick-red glob of water belched out, followed only by dry, metallic grinding.

Nearby sat a marble capital; the volutes and acanthus leaves carved into the stone made it seem like a gigantic albino plant. He assumed it was a temple piece dragged here by the house's owner to show off his wealth. Someone had once started a fire upon the marble's top. Charred coal remnants and gray ash swirled in small, airy eddies.

Rocky hills backed the broad ledge on which the house sat.

Except for the faintly humming sea and the path that led to the beach, there seemed no other way to the house.

Farther away, he was amazed to discover a creek running from higher in the hills down through the olives growing near the cliff. He cautiously peered over the edge, where the trees formed a natural fence against the drop. Before falling into the ocean, the creek filled a natural basin on a ledge.

A shirtless, young man was bathing only a few feet below him. Matthew clamped down a scream. He ducked behind a trunk and took a few breaths, and then peeked around again. The man still sat in the pool gazing out to sea—he wasn't an illusion.

He was the boy Matthew had seen in town last night. Sandals and a T-shirt lay neatly folded on a nearby rock. Matthew lingered for a moment, taking in the boy's shiny hair and rippled shoulders, and then crept back to the house.

He tried the pump again. It gave out a rusty dribble, which turned into a pure stream. He cupped his hand and drank. The water had the hint of iron, like the metallic taste of blood.

Matthew walked down to the beach. Seagulls cried and dove above. With a glance back at the house, he dropped his backpack onto the sand, took off his shirt and shoes, and waded into the surf. Cool waves splashed against his waist and up onto his chest. When he turned, the boy was on the shore, staring. He was sure this young man also remembered him.

Matthew left the water. "Am I intruding?" He stood over his pack now, ready to grab it and leave.

"No one ever comes here."

Relieved the man understood his Demotic, Matthew also wondered if that was a statement, or if it meant no one was supposed to come here.

The young man held out a jug, indicating Matthew should drink. So, he was welcome; the Greek custom of treating guests well still held in the young.

He uncorked the jug and took a swallow. Sour red wine made him grimace, but he covered it quickly with a smile. He handed back the jug. The boy drank also. Then they stood there at wave's edge. The boy was perhaps the most beautiful person he had ever seen, and Matthew felt uncomfortable with the way his shorts left him exposed.

He hadn't looked for a god, but he had found one.

48

"Are you hungry?" he asked.

"Yes."

They went up the slope to the old house, and Matthew spread a blanket next to the marble cap. The boy gathered scattered roof tiles, wood siding, and tree branches and pilled them in a mass atop the column piece. He lit the wood with matches from his pocket. They ate and drank wine mixed with well water.

"What is your name?" Matthew said.

"Stavros."

They passed the jug back and forth, watched the sun set, and fed the fire with sticks. When dark came, he told the boy about his flight from Athens. The young man grunted with what seemed amused agreement. "I have heard so too," he said. "It is ruined."

Eventually, Matthew unrolled his sleeping bag and lay down. The day had moved into cool evening. After climbing into the pouch, Matthew—strangely fearless, he blamed the wine and his fatigue—offered Stavros a space inside. Stavros slid in next to him. He smelled of pine and salt, and his skin was smooth and warm.

"Who lived in that house?"

"A ship captain. He was very rich."

"What happened to him?"

"He fell in love." Stavros stretched his arms towards the sky. "When it wasn't returned, he threw himself onto the rocks."

Matthew shivered. From this height, the ocean sounded like a hiss.

He woke once at the distant bark of the dog. Stavros was gone. Matthew must have just missed him; the sleeping bag was still warm where he had lain. Matthew fell asleep before he could think more about it.

Morning brought the heat again, and he drank deeply from the flow at the pump. There was no sign of Stavros, and even the empty wine jug had disappeared. He dove into the surf, knowing that swimming alone here was dangerous, even foolhardy. He paddled along the beach, past the end of the sand, until he came beneath the cliff where the trees grew. He climbed up the slippery rocks, bracing against waves that, threatening to knock him over, pushed at his legs, and located the trickle of water from the overflowing pool. He sipped from the water he caught in his cupped hand as it ran down the sea cliff.

Stavros was on the beach when Matthew returned, jug in hand. "I brought more wine."

While Matthew blew on the coals, Stavros wandered off to the pool. Fire self-sustained, Matthew also went to the pool. Stavros stood in the thigh-deep water, soaking and wringing his shirt, rinsing it of salt water. He splashed the water over himself. "Come down," he said.

Matthew did. Stavros kissed him. The water intensified the sensation of the boy's warm body. Stavros pulled away, climbed out, and put on his damp shirt.

The four young men Stavros was with that first night were at the camp site. When they saw Matthew their eyes narrowed.

"It's okay," Stavros said, using English, the first familiar words Matthew had heard in days, a reminder of the strangeness all around him, this foreign place and unfamiliar country.

They had brought wine, but no food, and eagerly and freely ate what Matthew offered. It meant he would have to leave tomorrow. Now that he knew the way, he could always return. Matthew was happy to keep these young men on his side. He sensed they were easily swayed into action—kindness or violence—the way young men can be when they feel strong and powerful.

Their speech was quick and full of idioms from some Aegean dialect. Much of what they said was unintelligible. Stavros left with them after mid-day, and Matthew roamed the hills behind the house. As he suspected, there was no road except for the path he came in on. He attempted to discover the source of the stream, but the water disappeared into the rocks as if emerging from blank stone.

On his way back to camp Matthew heard Stavros calling for him: "Where are you?"

Matthew ran until the house was in sight.

"I brought food," Stavros said. "For what my friends ate."

"Thank you."

Stavros turned to leave.

"Where are you going?"

"I'll come back tomorrow."

Too disappointed to say anything, Matthew watched Stavros cross the beach and disappear into the hills.

But Stavros returned the next morning. They swam to the spot where the stream fell into the ocean and then swam even farther, found a small shelf where they could rest. Drawn by Stavros's beauty, Matthew wished to touch him sprawled on the rock, touch his chest and brown nipples, his stomach and hips and thighs.

"Where are you from?" Stavros asked.

Matthew had difficulty recalling. Graduate school, his unwritten thesis, Gregory. Another life. Not remembering was so pleasant he felt transformed.

They washed in the pool. They started a fire on the marble cap. Stavros opened a can of calamari, looped the rings on a stick, and roasted them in the flames. He slid them off onto a tin platter and they ate. This time, they drank the wine undiluted. Above them the moon waxed almost full, and the glow of its white ribbon trailed on the water into infinity.

After the food was gone, Stavros sang. Matthew understood few words. Stavros gulped at his cup and then kissed Matthew, the wine taste strong and fresh in his mouth. They fell asleep on top of the sleeping bag.

When the dawn light woke Matthew, Stavros still slept beside him. He was thirsty and went to the pump. The night lay heavy in his head. No matter how hard he worked the handle the pump made only strangled, creaking noises. The wind, which had shushed through the olive branches these past days, was silent. Something made him stumble over to where the stream flowed. He found the track dry, the soil rocky and parched. The pool where he had bathed was an arid basin. Though the sun was still beneath the ocean, he noticed the air was superheated, like on a stifling summer day. His loneliness returned in a shock.

Stavros was at his side. "You must leave."

"I don't understand."

"My friends are coming to kill you."

A joke, he's making a joke Matthew thought, but he saw fear in Stavros's eyes.

The sleeping bag was already rolled and strapped to his backpack. The fire embers were cool and dispersing in tiny wind currents. Matthew pushed the moped down the slope, full of unseen ruts and bumps in the pale dawn. Scrambling noises were behind him, but no one followed. Stavros had disappeared in the shadows around the ruined house.

A dog barked above from the top of the rocks. In its rush

toward him, the thing's back legs flew over its head, and it tumbled down the slope.

Matthew kicked the moped alive and started on the path out. Barking sounded over the engine. Glancing back he saw a charging dog, lips curled away from white teeth. Another dog dove at him out of the scrub. He swerved just as it snapped at his leg.

Around a curve two more animals blocked the way. He steered towards them, angry enough he didn't care about running down the beasts.

They held their ground until the last moment, seemingly confident he would yield. Pain seared his ankle; a burning vise yanked his foot off the pedal. The back tire slid to the right, and he put out his foot to stop from falling. A large black dog held his ankle in its jaws, glaring up at him with a single, wild eye.

He punched the dog's ear. The animal yelped and released. It wobbled off, stunned. The other dog charged and he knocked it away with a bloodied sneaker.

Then he was up and on the moped. Barking continued behind him for a while, but was soon lost as he sped away. There had been those dark moments when he considered what it would be like to be dead. Though less irrevocable, his flight from home had been a substitute for death. Not a brave resistance against that desire.

Where the path joined the main road, he looked back for the house and olive trees, but failed to spot them. He continued on to town.

The grocer was quite concerned about his wound, and gave Matthew rubbing alcohol, bandages, and a glass of ouzo for his nerves. When he told him what had happened, told him about the old house and the olive grove, the man laughed. "That house was knocked down in a storm years ago," he said. "I remember. The day before the owner killed himself."

Matthew wanted to describe the boy Stavros, see if the man knew him, but decided against it. Gods bestowed joy and pain in equal measure. He couldn't help but wonder if in escaping his own destruction, he had also cast away his only chance for an exquisite release. He feared speaking of the boy would summon both upon him.

9. RESIDENTS OF THE INN
by Jessica Knauss

Dolores unlocked the closet door and pulled out the utility cart. A dull ache already radiated up her spine. Was she headed for the same place as her husband? A twinge, annoying but easy enough to ignore, until one day, she could no longer stand up straight. A gradual decline into the condition that would keep her motionless in that trailer all day, the monthly disability paycheck delivery her only way to mark the time. But no, Clay's weakness had come upon him suddenly. She hadn't even known there was an accident at the job site until the next morning, when he woke them both up screaming for the Lord to take away the pain.

She stooped to grab the crisply folded sheets and set them on one side of the cart, the bleached, raspy towels on the other. On each end, an empty sack, one for garbage and one for soiled linens. On top of the cart: bleach, boxes of soap, bottles of shampoo. Each item a pristine white; they betrayed any stray fluff or smear so the residents could complain to management.

The only bit of color on the entire cart was what waited inside the twin clear plastic spray bottles: a bright pink liquid, their all-purpose cleaner of carpet, tile, and toilet, of dust and biological matter. If only it would wipe Dolores's brain clean of thought. It was all she could do to make it through the day with that nagging voice in her head, telling her to stop complaining, that she should be glad one of them could still work, otherwise they might lose the trailer, too.

Steering the cart to the left, against its squeaky, protesting wheel, Dolores trundled to the end of the hall. She liked to begin at the high numbers so it was like a countdown. One hundred rooms before quitting time, fifty before lunch. Corporate's new policy to leave the empty rooms dirty until they were in demand only added to the work and made Friday the worst day of the week, easy.

A new resident in 125 helped by putting his dirty towels in the laundry bag and placing the new ones on his rail. He would never know the difference if she didn't change his sheets today. In 117, a little spider thought it could run across the couch without Dolores seeing it, but she sprayed the pink liquid to stun it and crushed it with a sopping rag. Room after room filled with people's night and morning rituals (or filth that had been left all week, and it was easy to tell), and at last Dolores stretched her back and got that strident popping. She wiped water and unidentified substances from her hands onto her starched white apron, and knocked on the door of 101.

A couple had lived in 101 for most of the year—they were definitely there by the time the flowers were out for spring. No matter what time of day, the wife's hair was perfectly in place, her outfit crisply ironed and coordinated. There was no earthly reason to look so nice if you never left your hotel room. Dolores had once walked in on some kind of internet video conference, so sure, maybe you should keep your upper half presentable, but the rest of you could be in pajamas and those faraway folks would never know. The wife would be that much nicer if she would relax a little, make herself at home.

Half the time, the wife had hung the "Recharging Right Now" sign and Dolores would have to remember to come back later, sometimes much later, long after her body protested that she was done cleaning for the day. If the sign wasn't up, most days the wife was there to open the door and insist that they needed no more than a few clean towels. That was fine to begin with, but over time, Dolores had stopped listening to the protests and changed the shower curtain or vacuumed the floor of her own free will. She could tell that the wife really wanted the bed made every day and the sheets changed at least twice weekly. The wife's protests served only to soothe her hotel resident's guilt. They all felt a tiny bit guilty for letting someone clean up after them, but then if things weren't spotless every damn day, calls would be made and the management would watch Dolores, who did not like to be watched. They would pester her until she was begging them to fire her.

But maybe in this case, no calls would be made. The wife was like all the others, but the husband was different. Dolores almost never saw him on weekdays, except at the breakfast bar, but without fail, he smiled and chatted and asked Dolores about her job. He looked her in the eye, unlike all these other businessmen, who seemed embarrassed to have to ask her about the airport shuttle or where the exercise room was. The other day, the husband even asked about Clay. Who was little Dolores that this important businessman should remember her husband's name? At Christmastime, he asked Dolores which days she had off, and on Christmas Eve, he handed her a gift card. He'd spelled her name wrong, but Dolores wasn't going to make a fuss about that when nothing like it had ever happened to her before. He also folded the linens, even the dirty ones. But she would always remember him as the one resident who treated her like a human being.

The door opened and the wife greeted her with a crisp northern accent, then returned to the work desk as usual, quickly absorbed into some kind of activity Dolores would like to be paid for, reading or writing. No more of this physical labor, this endless battle against other people's grime.

People should get paid according to how much actual work they do. Anyone who sits around all day like this wife should have to get up and earn her paychecks. In a world like that, Dolores and Clay would never have had to give up their house.

"What's the point of a trailer that's bolted down?" she'd asked, dreaming of driving all over this country, which someone had told her was big and beautiful.

"The point is a mortgage my disability can pay for," Clay had replied all too sensibly. That had been the first pang of regret Dolores felt about not having children. If only they'd had someone who could take them in… But it was too late. She would've had to do all the work, anyway, and now taking care of Clay was just like having a child. She probably hadn't missed much.

Dolores changed the bed sheets, switched out the towels, and ran the water in the bathtub for the wife to hear, then sprayed the pink stuff on the shower curtain and wiped it off again so it would make that loud scraping sound. The worst thing about this job wasn't the residents or the white linens or the management or even the nagging pain in her back. It was that even when you really cleaned something, it just got dirty again.

When Dolores came back out, the wife was already waving a hand to bid her good day, but Dolores let herself smirk. She wouldn't be gotten rid of that easily.

"You want some more soap, right? And shampoo, but not conditioner?"

After a few more tries, the distracted northerner understood and nodded. "My husband uses them. But not the conditioner." She had said the same thing most days for most of a year, reminding Dolores like she was some old timer.

"I'll have to go get some more. My cart's empty." Dolores remembered more about this couple than they would ever realize.

Without waiting to see if the wife understood her accent, Dolores stepped into the hallway, leaving the door propped on its chain. Headed for the supply closet, she braced her hands against the cart. Even without soaps and shampoos, it was heavier than before with the wet towels and wadded bed linens. When she leaned in to push, a sensation of downward movement came over her, even though the cart didn't budge. The carpet hurtled toward her and nausea made her squeeze her eyes shut. When she opened them again, the world was blurry.

No, not exactly blurry. More like eight focuses that ran together in colorless, grainy blobs. The carpet's pile seemed much more luxuriant than she would've guessed, and it was far too close. It smelled strongly of rubber and dirt and dead leaves. Although she lay on her stomach, it wasn't touching the floor. She flexed her legs and her whole body bobbed up and down. Pushups had never been this easy, even when she was a child. Had she had a stroke? Or had all those years of cart pushing given her superhuman powers? Dumbfounded, she tried to bring her hand to her forehead, but what came toward her without quite reaching was a thin protrusion covered in tiny black hairs. All that shaving and waxing, to end up a spider?

A great rumbling down the hall—Jake was coming with the laundry cart. "Dolores?" he called. He would have to get along without her for a moment. Right now, she had to figure out what in God's name was going on.

She scooted between the door and carpet of room 101 without

mussing a single one of the tiny hairs on her eight fast, supernaturally coordinated legs. The wife sat at the desk, absorbed at her computer, shifting slightly on the chair with casters. The woman would crush Dolores if she suddenly rolled back. Heart thudding in her… thorax, Dolores hurried to the corner near the door hinges. She would wait right here to catch her breath and figure out what to do next.

Lord, that carpet was nasty, striped in what Dolores remembered as brown, yellow, grey, and red, but now saw as shades of grey. Much worse than the carpeting in Dolores's trailer. What was the designer thinking? That it would hide the stains, pebbles, bits of food, loose fibers, and—oh, mercy!—the enormous, snowy skin flakes? Well, it didn't. Dolores feared she would be sick if she had to stay on that carpet another minute. The baseboard, covered in one color of carpet she couldn't identify, seemed a little cleaner—it didn't have dried leaves and stale popcorn, at least.

She lifted a leg, stumpy and spindly at the same time, and found that it hooked into the carpeting like Velcro. But she was able to move the leg just a little upward and remove it again, so, thank goodness, it wasn't a permanent marriage. Gingerly, she hooked both front feet into the baseboard and found that her other feet had followed without her bidding.

Was this what rock climbing felt like? Dolores had always wanted to try that. Step, hook, step, hook, and she made it to the part of the wall that was painted white.

When did the sheetrock get so holey? She found she could hang on here just as easily. But it had a colder feel that made her want to flee, and instinctively, she touched her bottom to it. When she lifted off again, a thin film attached her to the wall. She should have been disgusted, but it felt so exquisite, all she wanted was to do it again. She walked to the corner and deposited her film on the other wall, and soon, she had made a triangular web with loops and whorls like she could never make knitting.

The web was a natural white, not manufactured with bleach and tile and labels. She sat, contented, in the center of her web, causing only the tiniest sag. It was a good, solid house. A home. That was all she'd asked for, and now she had it. There weren't any dirty socks in a pile or dishes in the sink like there would be when she got back to the trailer.

Would she get home? Would she see Clay and fold his socks,

wash his dishes? Maybe she could scurry out to the parking lot and attach herself to someone's car, someone who lived near her, and leap off at the right intersection. Oh dear Lord, what a mess! She couldn't fold socks in this condition, any more than she could finish the first floor.

It had been nearly lunchtime when she'd entered 101. She certainly couldn't figure this out on an empty stomach. She crawled back to the edge of the web in the vague hope that some lunch would happen by.

And then a startling, thundering sound. The door.

"Hi, my dear." The husband's baritone vibrated along the web. The couple kissed. "Is Dolores here? The cart's outside."

"I don't know. It's the weirdest thing. She came in and did most of it, and then drawled something about more soap and shampoo for you, but she never came back. That must've been more than five hours ago."

Five hours. Lord, what a waste! And if the cart was still outside, what was wrong with Jake? And that probably meant no one had come along to finish this building, either. It would take all night if Dolores had to start again now! If she could start again now. She thought of Clay's face, usually unshaven those days, and a little bit ghoulish in the flickering light of the TV. The thing was, all that work sounded better than going back to the trailer. Then again, she might just stay right here, safe in her new house she'd built all by herself.

"That is strange. Dolores is one of the good ones," said the husband.

"I'm just the way God made me," Dolores would've said any other time.

"Hey," said the husband, rumbling Dolores again. "That little spider is back." He stooped near Dolores's web. "I'll never understand why he chooses to build his web back there. There are never any bugs in it." His breath rustled the tiny hairs on her body and she grasped the web fibers tight. Dolores had never noticed any spiders here when she was cleaning or she would have demolished them. Today it seemed like a really nice place for a web, but he was right. She might never catch dinner there.

He stood and turned away, only to return with one of the plastic cups from the bathroom and a note pad.

"Come on, little guy. You'll be much happier outside."

Dolores fled, but he was faster. The cup held her captive while he slid the notebook under, slicing at the ends of her legs just a little. That didn't hurt nearly as much as her back had, all that long time ago, when she was cleaning tubs and making beds. The couple's speech became muffled, back and forth, and Dolores hooked into the fibers of the paper while the husband lurched preposterously out the door, and then the light changed and they were out the other door. The cup was removed and the paper started to shake.

"Take it farther! Throw it in the pool!" the wife was saying.

But Dolores fell on top of a slick green leaf in the bush just outside the door.

"Thank you kindly," Dolores said, but the husband was already gone. She scuttled to the ground and hid behind the drainpipe.

When the time was right, she would sneak back into 101 and build another web, hidden behind the headboard. Dolores would protect that husband from the creepy crawlies that came in the night, and probably get a good meal out of it besides. Giant beetles with scary pincers, pregnant bedbugs rich with the blood of the sleeping wife, but none of the husband's, no sir, Dolores would make certain. She wasn't sure what would happen when the husband finally moved out of the hotel, as all residents must. For the time being, he was one of the good ones.

10. CHANGELINGS
by Elizabeth Nellums

I had not planned on taking my son with me to Landersville, and the
timing was inconvenient. I had been warned by the chair of my
department that I would need to publish a strong series of articles—
perhaps a book—to receive tenure at Ohio Valley, and the field
season was already foreshortened by the Methods and Analysis class I
had agreed to teach in August. But Adam was not doing well at
home, fighting with his stepfather again, and my ex-wife asked if I
could take him with me. It was not a request I could refuse.

By the way he slid on his headphones the moment we pulled out
onto the highway, I guessed he had no particular interest in
accompanying me, either. It was hard to remember there had ever
been a time he had begged to come to work with me.

This particular study I had set up with my old colleague Catherine
Dyer, with whom I had once co-authored a paper on the subcultures
of migratory farm workers. She was now mostly retired from
academic life, as her second son had developed what they call
"special needs," but she was still among the foremost experts in
mobile cultures, and was willing to share her research on the Scots-
Irish peoples of the Smokey Mountain region. They apparently
maintained a vibrant culture near her home in Landersville. I was to
join her for the next two months, then assume primary responsibility
for the analysis and publication of our research. It was her hope, and
mine, that we might be able to put together the definitive work on
the subject.

"They're almost certainly the descendants of the original settlers,"

Catherine had said, her enthusiasm obvious over the phone. "They're living entirely off the grid, but some of them still speak the old language at home." Truly, they did sound like a fascinating people. I agreed to come on the spot.

Following Catherine's directions, Adam and I drove down forested roads that I found suffocating, the branches overhead almost swallowing the car. I resorted to tuning into the public radio station, which, however, was soon cut out by interference from the mountains. Landersville didn't seem to be much of a town—it was discouraging that the GPS in my car couldn't locate it—but we persevered in silence.

At length we arrived at a scattering of homes tucked into the foothills of the National Forest. Catherine's comfortable-looking farmhouse was the farthest back from the road.

"You made it! Come on in. You must be exhausted. Don't mind the mess, right this way." Her hair was the same flame-red that I had remembered. Her elder boy, Matthias, ran out to see the car, hair as bright as his mother's.

"Be polite, Adam," I warned, for he was not disposed toward younger children—witness his constant fights with his step-brothers. "Catherine, this is my son, Adam."

"He's gotten so big!" she said. He shrugged and stared at the ground, looking put-out, as he had since he turned fifteen. "My younger son is inside," added Catherine, and I may have imagined the note of reluctance in her voice. "I have dinner ready, if you boys are hungry?"

We followed her into the house and were confronted with the second son, William, dull-eyed and vague. He must have favored his father; there was nothing of Catherine in his face, or his wheaten hair. "Hello, William," I said amiably, but he didn't acknowledge me in the least. He was sitting on the kitchen floor watching a drawer slide open and closed. It took me a second to see he was pushing it with his foot.

Catherine had put together a summer feast, and as we sat down to eat, she described her progress to date. "I'd been living here for years before anyone opened up to me," she warned, pushing a platter of fresh-sliced tomatoes toward me. "They mostly keep to themselves."

"How much do you know about the dialect?" This was a point of particular interest to me since I had first studied the patois of Jamaica.

"A couple phrases. They only speak it amongst themselves, and it's difficult to understand. There's a girl who brings eggs to the house who's probably your best chance to hear it. Her grandmother runs the main camp."

"I look forward to meeting her," I said, nodding encouragingly to Adam, who was eying William with evident distaste. Pulpy tomatoes slipped out of William's mouth, spilling over the plate. I looked away.

Catherine blamed the vaccines, I knew. *If you could have seen him before*, she'd told me once. *You wouldn't recognize him.* To me it was incomprehensible—a woman with her level of her education—but I said nothing. It was not my place to judge.

As it turned out, I had the chance to make contact with the subject group even sooner than I had anticipated. That night after dinner, as I was reviewing Catherine's meticulous notes, I heard a truck pull around the side of the house. I looked up to see a handful of children sitting in the back of a pickup, their bare legs hanging over the tailgate. They stared back with wary, unfriendly eyes. "They're from the camp," said Catherine in a low voice, waving out the window. "The girl in front is the one I mentioned." She opened the back door. "Rayanne, come meet my friend Michael."

I judged that she was about thirteen, a sturdy girl with dishwater blond hair that looked rather tangled and lank. She wore a pair of cut-off overalls over a checked shirt, and no shoes. Like the others, her face was rounded and closed-off, her skin burned deeply tan and rather dirty.

"Hullo," she muttered.

"It's nice to meet you," I said. "Miss Dyer says you come up here every summer."

Rayanne squinted up at me and shrugged. "Some," she agreed.

"R'Ann," rasped a low, distorted voice from behind me. I startled and turned around to see William, watching the stranger with intense, copper-penny eyes. I'd had no idea he could speak at all.

Rayanne met his countenance calmly. "'Lo, Liam," she acknowledged with a nod. That was it; they shared no other discourse. He turned back to the living room without a backward glance.

"An' who are *you*, then?" she inquired, and I realized after a beat that she was talking to Adam. I hadn't been aware that he was lurking in the door frame behind me.

"This is my son Adam," I said at once, drawing him forward. "Adam, come say hello to—Rayanne, did you say?"

"Tha's me," she agreed. "Adam." She bobbed her head.

Adam didn't respond, just examined her with narrowed eyes. To my surprise, rather than being offended, she smiled. "Would you like an egg?" She held it out to him in her dirty fist; it was light-blue, spotted grey, rather smaller than was typical.

"How pretty," I exclaimed. "Is this from a poultry stock you're cultivating?" I wondered if it might be an heirloom breed, perhaps one with history in the culture.

"It's one of our'n," she said, which was no answer. "Don' you want it, Adam?"

I thought he might refuse her, but after a long moment he extended his hand, silent. She dropped her offering into his larger palm.

"Say thank you," I prompted.

Adam said nothing, staring down at the bright-colored egg.

"Be seein' you," she said lightly, turning away.

"I know she's a little unusual, but she really is a wonderful girl," said Catherine, when I asked her about it later. "She's almost like a big sister to William—better with him than I am, half the time! They spend whole afternoons playing out back."

"She appears to have taken a liking to you, Adam," I observed, hoping I could draw him out with some innocent raillery, but he only glowered.

"Did she give you one of the eggs?" asked Catherine, knowingly. "William got one of those as a christening present, from the grandmother. They're pretty, aren't they?"

"I didn't recognize the breed," I agreed. "May I see it again, Adam?"

"She gave it to me," he mumbled, turning away and shuffling out of the room without another word.

"Honestly, I don't know what's wrong with that boy," I said, exasperated.

"Not to worry," said Catherine, smiling. "Children grow out of their little moods, eventually."

***

As it turned out, there was to be a lot of Rayanne over the next few days. There she was, sucking on a popsicle, watching Adam as he fiddled with the screen of his iPod. Refusing Catherine's marshmallow squares with a shake of her head. Singing tuneless and low as she unloaded boxes of eggs.

She was there the day Adam got a bee sting, offering to treat the wound with a dirty bag of herbs. "What are you using?" I asked, watching with interest as she muttered over the remedy. Having studied ethnobotany at Purdue, it was fascinating to find herbal medicine practiced here.

"Using?" She eyed me, sullen.

"Those plants—something you collected from up on the mountain?" They appeared to be the dried heads of what my mother called dog-tooth violets.

"Don't matter what the plant is," said Rayanne. "It's the prayer."

Adam shook his hand out, blinking. "It worked," he said.

"Rayanne, your gran is here," Catherine called. I turned and saw a grizzled old woman coming up the road, holding the hands of two little girls. Both were dirty and rough-looking, but I recognized the stringy fawn-colored hair.

"My cousins," announced Rayanne, following my gaze. It seemed safe to assume she had a lot of cousins.

"Strange lady, but very knowledgeable," Catherine had called the grandmother. "I managed to interview her once. William adores her."

I hadn't seen much evidence of William adoring anyone, but I took this on faith.

"Rayanne, do you think I could talk to your grandmother sometime?" I asked carefully. "Maybe we could sit down together and have tea."

Rayanne examined me with those oddly colorless eyes, and there was something a little malicious in her smile, or so it seemed to me. "I guess if you want, you could come up tomorrow," she said. "We'll have a prayer circle Sunday evening."

A religious ceremony sounded like a wonderful chance to observe the culture, and I couldn't be more pleased. My earliest breakthroughs with the Creole people in Haiti had been when I started attending their church services.

"You gotta bring Adam," she added slyly. "He need to walk with the Lord, it seem to me."

I wasn't sure how well Adam would respond to participating in an ethnographic study, but I said I thought it might be arranged. She nodded, then gathered up her rucksack and tottered down the front steps without so much as a wave goodbye.

The more I thought about it, the more excited I was that Adam would get to experience my work. Maybe it would give him a sense of direction, a feel for the college life on his horizon. That would be a relief for all of us.

He hadn't been enthusiastic when I described the invitation, but at least he'd agreed to attend. Catherine had excused herself, not wanting to contaminate my experience with any preconceptions, so it would be just us two.

"The important thing is to embrace the role of the impartial observer," I said, as we walked together up the dirt path to the camp. "It's not our job to apply judgment to any of the proceedings, merely collect data that can be used later."

"Uh-huh."

"Try to redirect any emotional responses; allow yourself to merely catalog what you experience."

I would have liked to elaborate, but Adam hurriedly walked ahead.

The homestead, when we reached it, was little more than a dirt yard, a scattering of chickens pecking hopefully at the dust. I could see a rundown cabin with a wide porch, set back against the woods, but somewhere there must have been trailers and vans. It seemed impossible that the whole group of them could live together in that one house.

There were maybe twenty people, all with Rayanne's same sullen look, gathered in a loose circle. A rawboned guitar was picking through the chords of *Here We Gather at the River* as we walked up towards the crowd.

The grandmother, Meriam, came forward to shake our hands and escort us to seats of relative honor on an old split log. "Miz Catherine's friends," nodded the old woman, shooting me a single sharp look.

"Miz Catherine's friends," I heard them murmur. "Welcome."

It was sticky-hot and so still that you could hear every sound in the forest around us. I went around the group introducing myself, while Meriam offered Adam a rather unappetizing hot dog. He ate, and the two of them talked together, a few words. He seemed on his best behavior, for once, and she placed one wrinkled, trembling hand upon his shoulder.

"Le'z give thanks," said the matriarch, and immediately several voices joined in a rolling, moaning chant, the words of which I could not determine. She raised a hand and everybody muttered *Amen*, then after a beat, began to sing:

I gotta home in glory land, outshines the sun—

The song seemed to continue longer than I remembered, and it seemed to me they were adding verses as they went. It shifted eventually to a new tune, the grandmother's voice like a raven croaking over everyone's.

Over yoon-der, go-o with Thee—

I could see Rayanne sitting with a cluster of her sisters. The little girls must have been coloring their hair with kool-aid, dark blue streaks that shifted among the dirty strands. They clapped their hands, keeping the beat as they lifted their reedy voices in a descant. The tune sounded strangely harsh as it lifted through the trees.

Cups of something were passed around, and I didn't realize until too late that whatever they were drinking was spiked with liquor. I saw that Adam had already finished his cup, but it was alright, I supposed; perhaps this would be a bonding experience, a funny story to tell later, how we had gotten drunk doing field research together. A real turning point in our relationship.

I was surprised to see Rayanne and her little friends drinking the spiked punch, they being not more than young children, really. But it was another culture, another way of thinking.

She was laughing at what might have been a little brother, dressed in clothes that were too large. When she felt my eyes on them, she hoisted the boy onto her hip and carried him away. A ragged child about William's age, with brilliantly orange hair.

He saw me watching them, and waved over her shoulder. He looked like Catherine's older boy.

There was more singing, faster and louder, and the little girls led the songs, their blue hair strangely bright in the twilight. I had meant to take notes, determine which individuals would be good subjects for an interview, develop the basis of an ethnography...but somehow I was caught up in the shrill music, and by the time I glanced down again at my notebook, I realized I had written nothing, though we must have been there for more than an hour already.

I hadn't seen Adam in a while, but he found me first, stumbling over to my seat. He knelt over the log, laughing and spitting into the dust behind us, and I put my hand on his back to steady him and felt the heat of him through his cotton shirt. "Easy, son," I said, but I was glad to see him enjoying himself. I felt closer to him than I had since I first moved out.

"They're *fairies*, Dad," said Adam, drunk and delirious from the heat.

I could hardly hear him over the noise. "What?"

But he had already leapt up, laughing, and was bounding away.

The quavering notes of a fiddle started up out of the darkness, building quickly to a dizzying speed. Then there was dancing, reels and quadrilles. The moon rose, dazzling bright, and there was more crooning, more praying, until the sound of frogs drowned out even the voices' song, and they began to break up, slipping away into the dark.

Suddenly I didn't recognize anyone, and all of the formless shapes were moving away.

"Wait," I said. "We need to get back."

I thought I caught sight of Rayanne, running with Adam hand-in-hand through the shadows of the trees, but when I called to them, I heard only my own voice echoing back.

I tried to follow, tripping over branches and roots in the dark, but lost the way. There was no one around me, no one ahead. Suddenly I couldn't even be sure how I had come—I looked back and saw only an empty meadow, wet with dew. No homestead, no dirt yard, no cabin.

I stood in the clearing and shouted for a long time, but there was nothing but the night creatures and the clouded moon overhead.

By the time I finally staggered home it must have been hours later, although my watch said barely any time had passed. "Catherine!" I shouted, as soon as I got close to the darkened house. "Call the police!"

I almost imagined I could hear the high, wailing note of the fiddle in the distance—or maybe it was a ring of laughter.

That imp was waiting for me on the doorstep, the boy William. He grinned at me—strange, ill-formed eyes—and pointed to their gift, propped against the door.

It was a wooden figure, built like a sawhorse in roughly the shape of a man. Blue eyes like my son's, painted above a crude smile. I could only assume it was offered in exchange.

I knew in that moment that Adam was gone.

11. THE CHAMBERS OF THE CANNIBAL QUEEN
by Constance Renfrow

Many years ago in the history of the world, there lived a king who married a second time. Above all others, the king adored his new queen, for she had hair as black as midnight and eyes as blue as the morning sky, and she sang the sweetest melody the world had ever known from the window of her castle chambers. The king spent every hour of every day tending to her every whim, but despite the king's devotion, she showed no love for him or his children—her three stepsons and single stepdaughter.

This last was a girl with eyes the color of the night sky, a complexion pale as the moon, and hair as golden as the stars themselves. And so it came that when the king died, the queen put the winsome little princess to work in the kitchens. The queen allowed the princes free reign of the halls, and as devoted brothers, they often came to visit their sister at work dicing meat and stirring pots, sharpening the kitchen knives and completing the meals the princes were to eat.

Every day the queen would sit in her window and sing, and she was never seen to eat or drink or ever leave her chambers. The princess and her brothers paid her haunting song no mind, but passing travelers would often stop to hear her beautiful melody. Men of all sorts—knights, princes, tailors, farmers—would knock on the castle doors and plead entrance to visit the enchanting beauty who sang so sweetly. The queen encouraged each man to enter, but the princess never saw anyone depart.

The years passed without any ceremony and with minimal joy,

and at last the eldest brother turned eighteen. A great change came about the youth. He walked about in a daze and his eyes reflected no light, and no longer did he come to visit his sister at her work. If he did talk, it was always in praise of "that beautiful voice," how lovely and good the singer was. One day, when the princess was hard at work and the younger brothers away on the hunt, the prince vanished. His brothers searched high and low for him, but could find him nowhere. And so the young princess made up her mind to ask her stepmother if she knew where he had gone. She went the queen's chamber and asked through the closed door:

"Stepmother, stepmother, we have seen neither hide nor hair of our dear brother. Where is it he could have gone, without a trace, without a song?"

To this the queen replied, "Without a doubt your brother has fallen in love, and has gone to seek his bride. Stepdaughter, stepdaughter, look for their return from your kitchen window."

The princess and her two brothers worried about it no more, and from her window above the washbasin, the princess awaited her eldest brother's return.

The next year, the middle brother turned eighteen years of age, and he, too, walked about as if he saw nothing, praised only the beauty of "that wondrous voice," and finally, one day, disappeared. The princess and her last remaining brother fretted over his absence, and so the princess went upstairs once more to ask her stepmother of his whereabouts. Through the door she cried: "Stepmother, Stepmother, we have seen neither hide nor hair of our dear brother. Where is it he could have gone, without a trace, without a song?"

Through the door, the queen answered, "Without a doubt your brother has fallen in love, and has gone to seek his bride. Stepdaughter, stepdaughter, look for their return from your kitchen window." Though with a heavy heart, the princess did as she was bid and resumed her perch at the window.

Finally, the youngest brother passed the threshold of eighteen, and he too became enamored of "that sweetest voice." His sister begged him to come to his senses, for she feared the loneliness of the castle, but to no avail. His eyes seemed faded, he heard not her pleas, and within days, he disappeared.

Once again, the princess turned to her stepmother for solace.

"Stepmother, stepmother, I have seen neither hide nor hair of my dear brother.

Where is it he could have gone, without a trace, without a song?"

The queen called out through the heavy door, replying as she always did, "Without a doubt your brother has fallen in love, and has gone to seek his bride. Stepdaughter, stepdaughter, look for their return from your kitchen window."

The princess cried bitterly upon losing her last remaining companion, and in her loneliness, she could only gaze from the kitchen window hoping to see her brothers coming down the road with their brides.

The years continued to pass by, friendless and empty, and yet the princess grew more beautiful with each day. She was so lovely that the sun and moon would weep to see her, for they knew they could not rival her beauty. Her complexion was as pale as the light of the moon, her eyes as black as the nighttime sky, and her hair golden like the stars.

One day as she looked mournfully out her window, a youth rode by on a brilliant white horse. So struck was he by her beauty that at the same hour of every day he would return to gaze lovingly upon the young servant girl—for that's how she appeared to him. Nor did his attentions go unnoticed by the object of his affections, for the princess adored the handsome youth and looked forward to the day when he would come to her window to speak to her.

This the youth resolved to do on his eighteenth birthday, and upon that day he returned to the castle at the hour of his custom. But this time, he was captivated by a voice so beautiful, singing the sweetest song he had ever heard, and lovelorn, he knew it to be his cherished servant girl. As he came to the kitchen window, he did not see her at her usual perch, but upon seeing a shadow at an upstairs pane, he knocked at the door. The most mellifluous answer bade him enter, and so he opened the heavy castle doors and followed the melody that drifted from upstairs.

The princess, who had been gone only a minute, spied her love at the top of the stairs, making his way toward the queen's chambers. Curious to know what business her beloved had with her stepmother, the princess followed at a distance—she was not so meritorious that she would not listen at keyholes. She drew nearer—and there the door slammed shut! As she crept closer, screams of horror pierced through the wood and rushed in a torrent down the hall. The princess raced to the queen's chamber and threw herself upon the ground, so as to peer through the crack beneath the door. The youth she loved lay upon the ground, his eyes empty, devoid of soul, and a shadow and a hem of richest silk indicated that the queen stood astride him.

The princess's heart ran still, but she allowed it not to stop, and pushing herself from the ground, she dashed to the kitchens she had so long been relegated to, where she knew she kept the knives sharp. The largest of these she pulled from its place upon the wall, and also a small silver fork, which she bent and molded so that one prong might serve as a lock pick. Her tools gathered, she sprinted again to where her lover lay insensible.

Echoing through the halls came the queen's sweet melody; it almost masked the bubbling of a cauldron and the sharpening of blades that served as harmony from behind the door. Again the princess peered into the confines of the room: there was no shadow to indicate her stepmother's position, nor could the princess see her lover splayed on the floor.

And so, as she had learned from her mischievous middle brother years before, the princess used the silver fork to undo the lock and opened the door as silently as is possible in old, creaky castles. Holding the kitchen knife before her, she crept into the room—the youth, she supposed, would be there and could quickly be roused. But what she saw was not so easily witnessed.

An enormous cauldron the size of a man boiled away in the sprawling fireplace, and butcher's knives and wrought iron ladles hung from hooks on the wall. Worse yet, the mantelpiece was built of bones and adorned with countless skulls; strips of beautiful, brightly colored fabric joined the pieces of men together. Three such swathes the princess shuddered to see, for she knew they had belonged to her vanished brothers.

The youth, her lover, was no longer upon the floor, but had been moved to a man-sized table with grooves carved along the margins— each one of them crusted with red. And there by the window, with her back to it all, the queen pored over an enormous, gilt-edged tome. The princess could do nothing but stare, and as the weight of what she gazed upon impressed itself upon her, she could not suppress the choke of horror that would have strangled her to keep silent. It grated upon the air and ceased the queen's song, for that creature turned slow around to look upon the intruder.

Stepmother made unhurried study of stepdaughter—of the girl's complexion pale as the moon, of the night-sky eyes that saw all but were so dark as to give no emotion away. Of the knife that stayed fast in unshaking hands. "My little child," the queen laughed, "can it be that you are not satisfied working in the royal kitchen? Do you come to work in my kitchen now?"

The princess only nodded her golden curls. The queen gestured toward where the prince lay and made a simple command: "Slaughter him for our stew." And her red, red lips curled with appetite.

The princess turned to her beloved and set herself between his body and the queen's sky-blue gaze. She raised the butcher's knife high in the air, and hesitating barely a second, began to sing as she thrust her knife down. "Stepmother, stepmother," her blade collided with a thud. "I see my brothers fell in love. I see they found their bride." The point of her butcher's knife had missed her suitor by barely a fraction of an inch.

"Stepmother, stepmother," the princess of the castle said. "It is done. My lover is dead."

"You have done well," the queen answered. And the man-eater stirred the contents of the simmering cauldron. "Now cut the meat into pieces so it can be cooked."

The knife rose again into the air, and again she sang, "Stepmother, stepmother, I see my brothers left some trace, I see their skulls atop your fireplace." And again the metal glimmered and shone and splintered the wooden tabletop. Again she did this, and again, as if she were chopping her lover into the littlest of pieces.

"Stepmother, stepmother, I know where my brothers have gone. They were lured here by your song."

At last, the queen whirled round to collect the first pieces of meat for her dinner, and yet, there was the youth still alive, still in one piece and breathing.

The queen shrieked a supernatural screech, and threw herself in a rage at her deceitful stepdaughter. But for this the princess was prepared, and she swung her sharpened butcher's knife at the man-eater's pallid throat. Again she swung—chanting "Stepmother, stepmother" at each vicious swipe, cutting through bone, through skin, severing at last the head from the neck, and both pieces collapsed in a pile upon the chamber floor.

The cannibal queen was dead.

The princess spun around to see her beloved, his skin spattered with the blood of his foe. The youth gasped awake, his mouth gaped open, and he surveyed the redness that stained the floor, the knife, the clothing of his lovely servant girl.

And yet he had only to stammer and stare, for the princess heaved the queen's fallen head into her own cauldron, and as she threw that vile burden, the cannibal queen's blood flecked the bleached bones that made up the gruesome mantelpiece. As though with the crash of thunder, the chambers began to quake, toppling the skulls from their resting place, and the bones tore from their fabric knots, pulled from their construction and wrecked upon the floor. Such a sanguinary bath could not but dye them incarnadine— saturated with redness and wet.

And as the bones clashed together, the room was filled with a brilliant light, piercing the couple's gaze and blinding them to the grotesqueries in which they were surrounded. When at last the light faded away, the princess and lover saw all before them, and a cry of joy escaped as one from their lips.

For there before them, sprawled, standing, gazing into the bloodied pot, were all the victims of the cannibal queen, restored to life.

"My brothers!" the princess cried, and she rushed to embrace the three resurrected princes.

And as the day turned into night and the sun passed down in the west, the brothers agreed their sister would be the first to ascend to the emptied throne, and her beloved would rule at her side, for that bold princess had rescued them all.

12. GEORGE'S DRAGON
by Clint Wastling

When Lavinia first asked George to create a large glass dragon, he refused. George was proud of his creations, some of which had found their way onto the polished mahogany surfaces of the great and good. The second time Lavinia asked him to create a ferocious dragon, she made him an offer he couldn't refuse. If he was willing, the day after she picked up the glass beast, she would marry him.

George was reluctant. "Why would you want to marry a middle aged man with hairs growing out of his ears and nose? And those on top of my head graying rapidly?"

"I don't know." Lavinia toured the man, examining him in the daylight of his high altitude flat. "You're not unattractive, and anyway, it's your character that counts."

"I've got plenty of that!" George replied, feeling quite elated. "Come and see me tomorrow, and I'll have plans drawn out."

Lavinia was delighted and kissed the artisan on the cheeks. George instantly reddened and stammered, "Thanks." Later, after the door closed, he realized he shouldn't be thanking Lavinia; it should have been the other way round, considering the creative energy he was about to expend.

George's high rise flat was one of the few in north Hull that hadn't been taken over by drug addicts and other even more unsavory types. There was some natural noise, but mostly when the lights flickered, it was George turning on his furnace and waiting to melt the strands of colored glass he relied on. Light-wise, the twelfth story was ideal. The windows faced north and east, providing an even light to work by and views over the distant minster towards the Wolds and right toward the distant sea.

George didn't expect the entry phone to beep. He pressed the intercom. "Hello?"

"Hello, my name's John d'Manio. I'd like to talk to you about Lavinia."

"Lavinia?"

"Yes the lady who's just left."

"Ok. Come up." George began sketching his ideas for a ferocious dragon. For several minutes he was lost to his creativity, but finally remembered his visitor. He was about to contact security when he heard a tapping at the door. George answered it cautiously, opening it a few inches before nearly closing the metal reinforced door on the gentleman to release the chain. The uninvited guest stood not quite five feet tall, and might have passed for handsome with his thin face and haunted blue eyes. The obvious only occurred to George after he'd invited him in. The young man possessed no lower legs, so his feet appeared attached directly to his knees.

"Please make yourself comfortable. Would you like a drink?"

"If it's no trouble, I'd like a tea."

George filled a kettle and produced his best china mugs. "How do you take it?"

"Milk only, I'm sweet enough already." George caught the flicker of mischief in John's eyes.

"Was it Afghanistan?" George pointed with the spout of the teapot as he placed it on the table between a menagerie of glass creatures.

"No, closer to home." The man didn't offer further elucidation.

"I live alone and have little money." George said after a long silence.

"I'm aware of that; I've made enquiries. I thought it wise after Lavinia's visit." The young man picked up a glass Pan figurine, his cloven hooves darker brown than his goat-like legs. The creature's torso was created with attention to musculature. He revolved the model created from finest Venetian glass, and George noticed the young man's manicured fingernails and slight staining, which he took to be chemical in nature. John returned the model to the table.

George was beginning to feel unnerved by his visitor, and wondered why he had consented to let him in.

"I might as well come straight out with it. Lavinia is a witch."

There was a long silence in which George remembered to breathe whilst staring at the young man. He picked up a glass character from his Wizard of Oz series. "This type: black hat, cat, and broomstick?"

"Precisely that type. But I don't expect you to believe me; you're a rational man, and you'll require evidence."

John balanced an ornately printed address card on Pan's outstretched arms. "Lavinia came to visit me. She said she had no money, but if I made her a ferocious dog, she would allow me to indulge all my passions. She was an attractive lady, so I consented. "

"How could you make a ferocious dog?" George asked, pouring the tea and passing over a mug of the brew.

"I'm a taxidermist. It's a misunderstood art these days. You should see my home, each room themed by my creations."

"Do you make money at it?"

"Indeed! A procession of elderly ladies pay well for their precious cats, dogs, rats and hogs to be preserved after their demise."

"Then you do better than me. Glass ornaments seem to have become unfashionable."

John sighed. "That is a shame. Do you mind if we watch the sunset whilst drinking our tea? I seldom get so great an advantage these days.

"Delighted."

George and the maimed young man stood at the window and watched the shades of pink turn red and the yellows become orange as clouds across the sky glowed.

"You were driven by lust?" George asked as he turned on the side lamp.

"I was indeed, and this was my punishment." He gestured his legs.

"What happened?"

"I told you, I am a taxidermist. She asked me to create a ferocious dog that she would set to guard her simple cottage in the woods. Lavinia told me she'd been plagued by hawkers, door to door sales, charity workers, and other miscreants. Her request seemed simple, and my payment a reward I longed for."

"I take it you did this for her?"

"Yes, I created a savage hound, larger than that which frightened Baskerville. It might have matched Cerberus for ferocity. Lavinia was delighted. She kissed me, she caressed me and made me promise to visit her cottage the next afternoon. As she lifted the straw and sawdust stuffed creature she flicked that card my way—that very one—with her address."

George pulled the curtains closed and further illuminated the room. "So you visited Lavinia?"

"Yes, I went to that cottage in the woods. As I approached, I heard the most savage of howls. The beautiful thatched cottage framed by hollyhocks and lupins possessed a vile guard dog. As I drew closer it salivated and bared its fangs, and I recognized the eyes first; they were the deep blue beads I had placed into the skull, only now they shone with hatred. This was my own creation set against me. Lavinia came to the door. 'What is it, Fluff?' Lavinia asked, though I shouted and waved. 'Tear off his legs!' she demanded. And so it did. It tore off my legs one by one and chewed off the flesh. I clutched my detached feet and pulled myself to relative safety. I remember nothing more until I woke up in hospital and the surgeon said, 'it was the best that I could do.' So that is how I came to be the man I am today."

"Your story is preposterous, of course."

John pointed at the card. "I'll take my leave now."

"Goodnight then." George felt he might have been rude in the haste he made to open the door, but the man had flustered and confused him. After he'd locked the reinforced door and set the chains in place, he turned off the lights and watched the world outside. Lights delineated streets and peered through curtains, but nothing could compete with the starlight except the distraction of the crippled young man shuffling along to a waiting taxi.

George didn't sleep. His dreams were filled with snarling dogs, dragons burning all he loved, and the beautiful Lavinia peeling away layers of clothing to reveal a body as sensuous as Lilith's. He woke with sweat cold on his skin.

He picked up the card and read the address. He typed the details into the satnav and waited: twenty six miles, forty seven minutes. He looked at the clock. He took a deep breath and began his journey.

Cold impressed itself on every window of his car. A dog howled. He looked up at the tower block and saw it as a functional concrete shell imposed on the neglected estate. The journey into the Wolds was quiet—a frightened deer, a running fox, ravens devouring road kill. He saw all of this as full daylight emerged, and then was diminished by the final valley. Here George was, robbed of sunlight by the trees crowding round the road. Stopping the car nearby he climbed out and investigated the drive. It meandered through the trees. There was no other sign of habitation. George avoided the gravel for the verge, preferring to approach quietly. In the distance a thatched roof could be glimpsed, then windows with curtains still drawn. He smiled and began whistling.

"Morning!" The paper girl sped past on her bike.

She startled him, and his heart pounded. He hid amongst the bushes as the girl peddled furiously away. A dog, chained by the garage, howled. Its eyes possessed a demonic light, which was enhanced by its black coat. George thought he could see flecks of sawdust on its legs, but before he could be sure, the creature pricked its ears and listened. It sniffed the air, growled, and ran at full speed toward him. George fled in terror, feeling his heart might explode. He regained the safety of his car and sat for several minutes recovering his composure before returning home. There were two possibilities: one, Lavinia was a witch who had somehow animated a stuffed dog, or two, the dog was real and John d'Manio was lying. George knew neither person, but out of the two, Lavinia promised the greater reward. Once safely ensconced in his flat, George began the designs for the formidable glass dragon. Its tongue would flick red and its scales would be opaline blue, which would shimmer to reflect the sky.

The entry phone rang, and he heard Lavinia's voice. "May I come up and survey your designs?"

"Of course." George pressed the unlock button and waited. He found himself pacing the room and biting his nails. Finally he unlocked the door.

"Why George, whatever is the matter?" Lavinia stroked his hair back in place and gave a loving peck on the cheek. He felt calmer.

"I've been working on these." He handed over the designs.

Lavinia looked through them. "Marvelous!" She said. "I'd like it to be six feet high."

George turned quite pale. "Six feet? That's a lot of glass. You could never lift it."

"I won't have to." She said with a cunning smile. "I'll just open the window and watch it fly away home."

"But a glass dragon can't fly." George said.

"I can bring anything back to life, make animate the inanimate."

"Surely not?" George felt the germ of an idea.

"Look!" Lavinia chanted a spell and the glass menagerie took life. "There's only one problem, the spell can never be undone."

"Never, surely not."

"Undoing the spell undoes the witch."

"Oh! And what would a witch want with a dragon?"

"It's to replace my dog, Fluff. He's showing signs of age, sawdust falling from his ears and tail. Soon, well, I fear the worst."

"Couldn't you have another made? I mean, a dog is less conspicuous than a dragon."

"You're right, of course, but a glass dragon would frighten off everyone and never wear away."

"But it could be smashed or melted."

"Precisely. When can I expect to take delivery?"

George thought about this; he did a calculation. "A month. However, there's one special request. Can you make a dragon live without seeing it?"

"Of course, yes. But it's a strange request."

"It's to spare my feelings, in case you don't like it."

Lavinia smiled. "Anything for my future husband."

"Thanks." He escorted Lavinia to the door and waited for a kiss, but in vain—Lavinia just patted him on the cheek and skipped down the corridor. George began to work on the dragon, starting with its great brown talons. Later he added wings as blue and specular as an opal. All the time the ornaments that Lavinia had animated helped carry materials and clean up.

John rang the intercom. "Any chance of a visit?"

"I've been waiting for you." George said, and came out into the hall to meet the young man. John made an effort to walk, but his gait looked painful and more of a waddle. He gave out a sigh of relief when he sat down. "That's some change," the younger man remarked on seeing the glass creatures playing on the coffee table. He picked one up to feel how it had become living material.

"I have to confess, I didn't believe your story of a stuffed dog that returned to life, nor did I believe in witches, until Lavinia came to see the progress on her glass dragon."

"You are determined on making that aberration for her?"

"Quite determined; you should always give a witch what she wants."

"Or you never know what revenge will be extracted." John pointed to his legs.

"So I have a plan. Come with me."

Instead of a dragon emerging from Venetian glass, two perfectly formed legs waited. "I need you to try them on, and there's a few finishing touches. What do you think?"

"Think? I'm overwhelmed. No one has ever done anything so nice, but how will you get Lavinia to animate them?"

"I've asked her to cast the spell before seeing the dragon."

"Clever. And afterward?"

"Well." George touched his nose. "Let's wait and see."

George completed the legs and began work on the dragon. The beast frightened its creator with its large fangs and flesh ripping talons. With only a day to go, George borrowed a surgical screen, moved his scaly creation behind it, and stood in front. The screen did its job.

"I'm sick with every type of nerve," John said.

"That's how I feel, but there's something else as well."

"Something else?" John asked.

"Yes, I believe I've found a friend."

John colored a little. "I thought the same but didn't dare to hope."

"Have you thought of living by the sea?"

"Yes, I'd love to. Let's see if we survive the next couple of hours. An angry witch might do anything."

"She might. I'll reason with her, and besides, I haven't broken my bargain." He peeled back the screen and heard John's intake of breath. The dragon stood on its hind legs with talons ready to strike, except that he'd been given a top hat and cane to carry.

"Frightening but urbane," John said after some thought. He was interrupted by the doorbell.

"Right, you assume your position in front of the dragon. Keep your fingers crossed."

George felt his heart race. He unbolted the door, where Lavinia stood wearing her finest black outfit. She pushed past the glassblower.

"I'm eager to see my creature."

"Remember our deal."

"Believe me, I remember."

George stood Lavinia in front of the screen. "Well, it's down to you now."

The glass ornaments strained to see the events from the coffee table.

Lavinia closed her eyes, took a deep breath, and exercised her fingers. She intoned some words and wiggled her little finger; there was a pause, and she repeated the spell. The air in the room crackled with static and daylight appeared to be sucked out of the sun and pulled into the flat. George wiped sweat from his forehead. There was a scream. The screen fell forward. A tall thin man stood, finding his balance on restored limbs. He stretched and pointed to his feet. "Perfect, George."

Lavinia went pale, then pink, and finally an unhealthy shade of violet. Her eyes widened in anger. "You've betrayed me!"

"No." George said calmly as the witch's fingers twitched. "There is your dragon, and may you be happy together. I absolve you from your bargain."

"You absolve me!" The air cracked and her little finger flexed. She intoned a spell and cast it. For a moment John stood transfixed as the energy swept around him. There was a second scream.

"Tricked! Tricked! I am undone." And so she was. Her body unzipped top to bottom, front to back. Her insides became her outsides, and finally vanished with an echoing cry.

"Are you ok?" George asked.

"Ok?" John moved his legs, knees and ankles. He grabbed George and they danced around the coffee table.

"We did it." George said.

"No, you did it." John added and planted a kiss on George's lips. There was a long moment of silence before George replied. "I hope you'll do that again sometime." They both laughed and threw themselves on the sofa. It was only when they paused for breath that the movement of scaly feet and tail were heard.

"And what about me?" The dragon asked. "Don't I get a happy ending as well?"

13. CHILD OF THE RIVER
by Anne E. Johnson

Jin Kyong was an old woman. She'd been a fisher all her life, as her mother and father had before her. The village folk liked to say that she kept herself to herself, spending the first few and the last few hours of each day's sunlight alone at the river's edge with her poles and nets.

That's why nobody else saw the baby.

Now, Jin Kyong had heard the stories of her people, so she knew how the girl Sim Chung had swum long and deep to plead that the river dragon restore her father's eyesight. That was a wonderful story. But, to Jin Kyong's mind, what came before her was even more miraculous. This baby was too small to swim. She floated on the water. As the current drew her closer to the dock where Jin Kyong sat, she saw what kept the child buoyant: a hundred silver trout circled rapidly beneath her tiny body, turning the water itself into a boat.

Jin Kyong lifted the infant girl from her burbling cradle. "Hello, child of the river."

The baby smiled at her, showing her shiny pink gums.

Having never found a husband, and being solitary by nature, Jin Kyong knew nothing about raising a child. So she bundled up this baby birthed by the waters and took her to the village center to find her a home.

"We can barely feed our own children," some villagers said.

"We sleep four to a bed already," said others.

But the most truthful among them said, "She came to us by river magic, so she may carry a curse."

Like all the villagers, Jin Kyong believed in the river's magic, but she had never thought of it as a malevolent force. She'd learned to trust the river, and to let it keep those secrets that humans weren't meant to know. She couldn't believe this beautiful child might be anything but a blessing.

"I guess you're stuck with me." Speaking softly, Jin Kyong kissed the swaddled girl on the brow. "Perhaps it's fate. After all, neither of us has any teeth. I shall name you Bounty, for never has the river given me such a gift."

The baby cooed, and Jin Kyong lost her heart to her completely. She had never before given her heart away.

For the first year, Jin Kyong fed Bounty on goat's milk and traded the fish she caught for new, soft blankets and ever-larger clothes. The child never made any sounds, although her face would show pain and joy, and her shoulders would shake with weeping and laughter. She and Jin Kyong were never separated. When she fished in the morning and evening, she carried her in a fur-lined creel. Although she could not hear her, Jin Kyong saw that she cried every moment she was fishing, and only smiled when they'd come back to her cottage.

After a year, she figured the baby was done with milk. She fried up a walleye in her ancient iron pan and blew on a steaming spoonful until it was cool. But Bounty would not open her mouth, and her face creased with misery.

"You'll like it," Jin Kyong said. "It's nice and mild. You must eat real food, or you'll get sick, my dearest Bounty."

But she wouldn't eat it, or even look at Jin Kyong. Tears made her eyes red, and Jin Kyong's heart ached. Finally she got her to eat some bread and stewed greens. She even smiled a little, and the old woman sighed with relief.

Another year went by, and now Bounty began to do more than cry when Jin Kyong fished. When she took the child to the river, she would clap her hands or move Jin Kyong's pole around to scare away the trout and steelheads. On those rare days when she did catch something, the child would cradle and stroke the wet fish, kissing it tearfully.

"Come, now. Give it to old Jin Kyong," she would coax.

But Bounty would look at her defiantly, and with her tiny

porcelain hands, she would pull out the hook and throw Jin Kyong's dinner back in the water.

The old woman learned to live on bread and stewed greens. But she needed a few fish to trade in the village, and Bounty wouldn't let her catch any. As the next year rolled past, it became harder to get the basics they needed to live. Jin Kyong spent all the coins she'd saved in the jar in her window box, and now had no way to buy bread.

"Oh, what shall I do?" she asked the river. "I must fish to survive, but I cannot bear to make dear Bounty cry. What will become of us?"

As she wept selfless tears into the rushing water, she noticed a school of steelheads collecting at the bank, bucking the pull of the current. Jin Kyong's instinct was to reach out and catch one in her bare hands, but she stopped herself when she noticed that the fish were doing something strange.

With their snouts, the steelheads dug in the pebbles in the river basin, poking and poking until growing clouds of silt obscured their work. It seemed to Jin Kyong that they were searching for something. Soon she saw a bright yellow glint on the water's surface, although the sky was overcast.

"What is that?" she said. "It looks like gold."

Indeed it was gold, a single gold piece held in a fish's maw. Jin Kyong reached out and gripped it in her fingers. Then, in an instant, all the fish swam away, and she was left with a sum large enough to keep herself and her beloved Bounty fed and housed for weeks. The old woman got down on her old knees and rummaged around in the riverbed for more coins, but she found nothing but useless stones, slimy with algae.

After the moon had waxed and waned twice, little Bounty came to Jin Kyong's side and showed her the ripped seam in her dress. Once again she had outgrown her clothes, but Jin Kyong shook her head.

"I'm sorry, dearest. We haven't enough money to buy you a new frock, nor even to buy a piece of cloth to sew into this one."

Silent Bounty, still just a child, took the old woman's gnarled finger in her soft, fleshy hand and led her to the riverbank. Again the steelheads dug among the pebbles. Again a fish emerged with a gleaming gift in its mouth.

And so the steelheads presented Jin Kyong with one gold coin every two months. Once, and once only, the old woman got greedy and spent her money in a single moon's cycle, but the fish wouldn't give her any more gold before it was time. A desperate Jin Kyong scooped great handfuls of soil from the river, hunting for the source of the treasure, but never found it. She had to find a way to get by until the steelheads brought her another coin. Feeling foolish and ashamed, she sold a chair that had belonged to her own mother. From then on, she practiced greater prudence and gratitude.

As for Bounty, who had caused all this change in Jin Kyong's life, she grew up healthy of body and calm of spirit. The villagers all thought she was strange, and told Jin Kyong so. True, she walked a bit funny, as if uncomfortable on her legs. True, she never learned to talk. True, she held her eyes open unusually wide and rarely blinked. True, when she was around people who talked loudly, she would dart away. But Jin Kyong thought she was perfect.

When she swam she really was perfect, not like a human at all, but blending in with the silver shimmers of pike and bass. Sometimes she would be under the water for so long that one might think her drowned. But Jin Kyong knew better. She knew that the fish would protect her daughter, as they always had.

Often Bounty would urge Jin Kyong to swim with her, yanking at her arm. Her ancient, aching joints couldn't flit and squirm through the current like Bounty's, so she would simply stand in the water, letting it flow around her. She loved the thousand sensations this brought, reminders of her vital youth. She cherished the tickle of fishtails against her belly and back, the poking rocks under her feet, the silver flashes through the murk, the mossy scent of river mud.

And so it went on for seventeen years, as these two cared for each other and the river cared for both of them. Day by day, young Bounty grew and flourished, and old Jin Kyong shrank and dried, as is the natural course of living things. Just as Bounty stopped needing the aging one's constant protection, Jin Kyong began to need hers. Dear Bounty nursed Jin Kyong as her arms and legs weakened, her breath became shallow, her skin translucent. Finally Jin Kyong knew that her path through this world had ended.

It was a struggle to lift her hand, to beckon Bounty to her. Bending down next to her bedside, Bounty put her ear to Jin Kyong's mouth to listen. "I am old," she whispered, "and I am dying."

"You are young," Bounty whispered back, the first words she had ever spoken, "and you shall live forever."

Jin Kyong felt her brittle body lifted in Bounty's arms. She was not afraid of death now, since she faced it encircled by Bounty's love. When she bore the old woman to the water's edge, Jin Kyong was grateful to pass her last breath looking at this river that had given her so much.

But when Bounty waded into the water, Jin Kyong became alarmed. She wheezed and stuttered.

"Hush," Bounty said. "I shall make you mine now, just as you made me yours."

Deep, deep, into the rolling brown-green water she dipped Jin Kyong, orbited by a hundred mercurial fish. Jin Kyong felt herself become one with the river, and thought she must now be seeing the ever-moving water as the fish saw it. In wonder, she watched as her frail limbs grew plumper, her spine straighter. She could feel new hair pushing through her scalp, and the water played with it, swishing the strands from side to side.

Bounty pulled Jin Kyong upright, and the once-old woman stood strong on her own on steady, muscular legs. She saw the sunshine glisten against her newly youthful breasts as the fishes nudged gently at her waist.

For the first time, Jin Kyong noticed Bounty's blossomed womanhood with a special sense of wonder, and Bounty, in turn, seemed to look at her in a new way. Leaning forward, Bounty touched her lips to Jin Kyong's, and wrapped her arms and legs around her, pulling her into the eddying flood. Water, fishes, and limbs intertwined blissfully. As one with the current they flowed downstream, and Jin Kyong knew that this child of the river would take her to an eternal paradise.

14. CINDERELLA AFTERWARDS
by Misha Herwin

It's never easy being the child of a single parent. You are either the center of attention or a rather inconvenient fact to be glossed over, or ignored, as the situation demands.

My father fell into the second category. When my mother died giving birth to me, he withdrew into the castle library, where thick walls shut out the cries of a tiny, bewildered baby.

While he immersed himself in his studies, I grew up in the care of the servants. My playground was the kitchens and gardens of my ancestral home; my best friend and companion was Buttons the boot boy.

By the time I was twelve years old, I was a strange, uncouth little being with few manners who loved animals and books. I also had a talent for numbers and doing accounts—the result of being taught solely by my father's steward, who had made it his responsibility to give me at least a basic education.

It was at this point that my father stumbled out of his haze of grief and realized that something must be done about this wild creature who was his daughter, so he married my stepmother.

Contrary to the stories that were later circulated about her, she was not a cruel, vicious woman, but a fat, comfortable, middle aged, middle class matron who never understood the ways to the nobility or why my bookish father preferred to spend his time in his library rather than strutting his stuff at court.

She also had two plain, not ugly, but silly daughters to provide for, and she thought that marrying my father would give them a better chance of snaring a wealthy husband. What she failed to see was that in spite of the castle and land, my father was no longer rich. The long years of seclusion meant that his estates had been neglected, and in spite of all his steward's efforts, his income had dwindled year by year.

In the first few months of their marriage, my stepmother did her best with me, and I did try, but I found my stepsisters, with their obsession with ribbons and laces and their fearsome appetite both for sweetmeats and court gossip, stupid beyond belief. They bored me, as did the endless lessons on etiquette and who was who in the great families of the land. I soon went back to my old ways, sitting by the fire with Buttons while Cook told tales of demons and goblins and we laughed and shivered with fear.

In despair of my lack of improvement, my stepmother gave up. She told my father I was stupid and badly behaved and there was nothing to be done with me. Whether my father believed her, I do not know. By now he had retreated back into the sanctuary of his books, and less than a year after the marriage, he fell sick and died.

He left everything to her, of course, with a sum set aside for the dowries of his daughters. Not that there was any gold left. All we had was gone.

My stepmother was furious. With my father, with fate, and most of all, with me.

Declaring she could not bear to set eyes on me, I was banished to the servants' quarters and told I would have to work for my keep. Not that I minded. Buttons and Cook were still there, though in a fit of temper, my stepmother had dismissed my old teacher. As time went on, the rest of the servants left. Even Buttons talked of making a new life in the city, and Cook grew old and frail.

I did my best—swept floors, lit fires, heaved buckets of water from the well, even turned my hand to cooking. Not that I ever got any thanks for my efforts. Just a constant flow of insults. Cinders, they called me, taunting me about my dirty hands and face, my increasingly ragged clothes. My stepmother would have beaten me if I'd kept still long enough for her to catch me.

In spite of all I could do, the castle grew colder and darker with each passing year. The roof leaked, cobwebs shrouded distant turret rooms. Unpolished floors warped and creaked. Mice ran riot in the pantry and the books in the library turned green with mold.

There was still some warmth and comfort to be had in the kitchen. Buttons kept us well provided with wood for the range, and I found a cache of my grandfather's best port deep in the recesses of the cellar.

We were sharing a bottle one day, Buttons and I, when he rummaged in the pocket of his coat and pulled out a crumpled piece of paper.

"This came for you," he said.

"Another bill." I was about to thrust it into the flames when he snatched it from my hand.

"Don't do that. Look. It's got the royal crest on it."

It was an invitation to a ball at the Royal palace. All unmarried ladies of noble birth were invited, in the hope that the heir to the throne would finally chose a bride.

"They've got one too," Buttons said, jerking his head in the direction of my step-sisters' chambers. "Don't think they stand much of chance though." He held out his glass.

"Nor do I," I said, pouring the rich red wine.

"Shame," Buttons sighed. "You could have married him and I could have been your Lord Chamberlain, or master of your household, or—"

"—Or slayer of the royal rats, or cutter of the royal wood, or rubber of the royal feet," I giggled. These were but some of the duties he now filled in our household.

Buttons slapped his thigh and laughed, and we went on adding to the list until the last of the port had gone and we staggered off to our beds.

I woke to a pounding head, a dry throat, eyes that felt they'd been scoured with sand, and a deep feeling of injustice.

What money she could scrape together my stepmother spent on her daughters' outfits for the ball. They had new gowns, the finest kid gloves, satin slippers, and painted fans. I had nothing.

"After all, who would want a dirty little thing like you?" my stepmother said when I raised my right to be included in the invitation.

"It's not fair," I said as we sat in the kitchen on the night of the ball.

"Nothing's fair," said Buttons, and reached for the bottle of port.

"Stop that this instant," a voice rang out, followed by a blinding flash of light that sent the mice scuttling back into the safety of their holes.

My fairy godmother had arrived, and duly worked her magic. Dressed in a cloud of white silk, shimmering with diamonds and pearls, I rode in a glass coach to the palace.

The prince was tall and blond. Handsome and charming. His eyes were blue, his lips red, and he showed great interest in my tiny glass slippers, which were far more comfortable than they looked and showed my little pink toes to great advantage.

Unlike satin or velvet, however, they slipped easily from the foot, and I lost one as I ran at midnight from the palace. It did not break, however, and now the reunited pair take pride of place in the royal collection of shoes.

My husband, the crown prince, owns more than a thousand. He and his companion, Duke Dandini, Lord of the Bedchamber, spend hours with their shoes.

We married in great splendor, my stepmother and sisters almost perishing with bile and venom. I gave Buttons a position in my household, but he soon eloped with a duchess, and he and his lady love rapidly got down to breeding a fistful of heirs.

The royal cradle, however, remained empty. The Queen, my mother-in-law, grew more and more pointed in her comments about my health. She was always asking whether I felt sick in the mornings, or suffered from any unusual cravings. She even took to questioning my maids about the state of my underwear.

When the whispers began about the dangers of inferior bloodlines, of not choosing a bride from a royal house, I knew that something had to be done. Somehow or other there must be a royal baby.

I could hardly broach the question with the prince, who after kissing me on the cheek had spent the rest of our wedding night snoring softly on the other side of the bed. Buttons had gone from court, and there was no one else I could trust.

I was contemplating stealing my share of the royal jewels and running off to foreign lands when my fairy godmother arrived, bringing with her a handsome young footman.

"He's a good lad, one of mine, and I'm sure he'll prove satisfactory," she said before vanishing.

Left together in my chamber, my new footman certainly gave

satisfaction.

When it was announced that I was to bear a child, there was great rejoicing throughout the kingdom. The king and queen could not have been kinder. I was showered with gifts, my every wish was granted. As for the prince, my husband, he and Dandini designed the most exquisite nursery suite for the new arrival. Cradles gowns, swaddling bands, teething rings—they spent hours debating over every little detail.

Luckily any female processes are more than their delicate natures can stand, because otherwise, it is doubtful that the baby's tail and whiskers will escape their scrutiny. However, with a little plucking here and a sharp cut there, I think my bonny bouncing boy will pass muster.

15. WHEN THE SKY BOWED AND NAMED THE SEA
by Chris Blocker

These are the annals of my transgressions. Word for word, this text—accurate in every detail—could never convey the truest feelings I have packed deep within my damaged soul. Not even the gods, in all their greatness, could craft the words to express the fury that rages within me. My finite mind, battling emotion, struggles to concentrate on the reality of it. Could these words truly release the shackles that enslave me? It matters not. If nothing else, I owe an explanation to the voices that will find me, even in my isolation. Perhaps here, in these jots and tittles, I can find solace from the cacklers demanding proof that I loved him. Proof that I did not set out to kill my son. Therefore, I present these chronicles—my fall from grace—for all the world to see.

There is no need to relive the incident at the Acropolis. The story has circulated so many times that it has taken on a life of its own. My version of the facts would only complicate matters further and detract from the necessity of this story. I am no stranger to falling—I assure you Talos fell, as did Herse and Aglaulus before him. My mention of the death of my nephew in Athens is instead the catalyst for the rest of the events as they happened; it was that moment of unrestrained jealousy that brought me there to the island of Crete. For it was on that island that destiny took an unexpected twist.

Some have said I fled to Crete so I could offend the king; rather, truth be told, I had hoped I would find his favor there. After divulging my intellect and soul into the carcass of his feeble, gray courts, one might imagine that I would have become heir, not imprisoned. A lapse of judgment, the result of an appeal to my weaker sensibilities made by two young lovers, was all it took to change my fate; I had given the couple means of escape and the freedom to live. The king was angered, and I was forced into the complexities of my own mind: the labyrinth. This was my inescapable masterpiece—my madness. I knew the king's reputation, but I did not expect this punishment. Along with my guiltless son, imprisoned only because of his connection to me, we found our residence within the arteries and veins of the maze.

"So dark," my son said, his eyes still adjusting to the lack of light. "So drab. I don't like it."

"I don't intend for us to reside here," I said.

He ran his hand along the walls, then looked at his hand as though the mysteries of such a place might now be lodged in the swirls of his fingertips. "What sort of person makes such a place?" he asked.

I jumped to curse the boy, but reason found me first. I knew he meant not the architect of the labyrinth, of course, but the person who ordered its creation. There is no fault in the craftsman who takes orders from the overseer, only in the craftsman who assembles a shameful construction. And this labyrinth was built of the finest quality; I had done the job I had been commissioned to do. Perfect. Inescapable. Deadly. "How do we emerge from here alive," I said under my breath, not intending an answer.

"Why don't we find the exit?" he asked. "You said this was a maze; therefore, there must be a solution."

"No, that won't work. Minos has the portal guarded."

"Then it's not a maze, but a prison."

I quieted him, told him I needed to contemplate the matter. He responded by sidling down the corridor, sizing up the towering gray walls. If I'd known then what I do now, I would've responded differently. I'd have let him share his naïve thoughts. The only thing I gained by dismissing him was expediency. Fate was waiting just outside of those walls, and I sent time hurtling forward by telling him to be quiet. If I'd known then... alas, I have yet to invent the machine that can glimpse the future.

We made residence in a damp, dirty room built atop of the labyrinth overlooking the Cretan landscape. Too high above the valley to escape, yet close enough to serve as a reminder of the world below, our asylum served as our tormentor. I spent the days searching my troubled spirit, while my son quietly stained the walls with childish figures. His distraction and his silence angered me, but I refrained from showing it. Instead I let my mind loose in the halls of the maze, searching for a solution. Eventually, it circled back in on itself, and for once, I was lost. Before me, on the walls, was a creation of magnificent scope. No, the drawings were juvenile, lacking any sense of artistry or life, and the brushes he had used rudimentary at best, but the colors! My mind had been responsible for elaborate mechanisms, inventions that bridged earth and the heavens, even life, but never color. Here were dyes of the most intricate colors—colors I had no name for, but wanted to learn.

"Have you assigned names to these colors?" I asked.

"Yes," he said.

"What do you call this one?"

"Psammorosia," he said.

"And this one?"

"Chionokrys."

I pointed to another and he said, "Portokáli."

"A fruit? No, portokáli doesn't seem right," I said. "What about... perihelion?"

"Portokáli," he said, not taking his sight from the color on the wall. "Or, if you prefer, portokal-*ís.*"

I shook my head and declared my son an idiot. I had no time to waste on the ridiculous names of made-up colors. Time was running away; we had to find a way out. I set my mind at the beginning of the labyrinth and ran through it again until sleep caught me.

I woke to the orgy of light that pushed its way through our window. In an instant, I found myself peering out at the monochromatic sky—a sea of orange. Portokalís. I remained there for hours while my son slept.

A small bird, a hawfinch, I believe, flittered by the window, and my soul followed it, flying in the expanse of my son's brilliant invention. I closed my eyes and inhaled the most refreshing, pure air my palette had ever tasted. Once this labyrinth had contained a beast misunderstood by men; now it held a son misunderstood by his father. Alas, that was it!

"Our salvation!" I exclaimed with a shout, waking my son, to whom I explained the whole thing. Hurriedly, we began our work. I made plans and built, while he gathered the materials. Soon, I would inspire a world of flight. We would. My child would carry on my legacy after all; his name would be remembered.

It took two weeks of labor to achieve our goal. We removed beams of wood from the inner sanctum of the maze. Although easy to locate, we found our task of removing the lumber in operational pieces to be difficult. Luring birds was much easier than I had speculated. Only needing the asymmetrical flight feathers, we devoured the rest of the fowl. Perhaps the most strenuous part of building our invention was finding an agent that would hold it together. I have already heard the rumor of angels saying that it was tar that held it. Truth is, there was only so much tar that could be found in the labyrinth. We dug deep within dark crevices to find anything sticky. Largely, we took from the remains of the Minotaur— that perverse ingenuity of my own and of Pasiphae's grotesque desires—and drained it of its natural adhesives. It was far from perfect, but it should've held long enough for us to find freedom.

Finally, our perseverance paid off. We looked at the miraculous feathers of protein and water held onto the delicate frame and knew history was about to be made.

The next day, I tested the wings, jumping down from the high window onto the floor below; the testing ground was insufficient, but it served its purpose. I told my son about the art of flying and the limitation of our wings. He nodded, and without asking any questions, said that he understood. My gods, if only I could've made him understand. His eyes fixated on the window; his heart had already made the leap. So, after giving one another an honest smile, we walked to the entrance of the free world and jumped.

What followed happened in the blink of an eye under the intoxication of adrenaline. Although shaky, I was flying! Indeed, the miracle had unfurled! We made our trek against a sky of quickly forgotten, fragile hues. I remember my mind rushing with the thoughts of what new heights this discovery would bring me to. I remember thinking about the endless possibilities. And I remember a scream from behind as my only child began to fall. At a rate of nearly ten meters per second, he made his descent back to the earth. I had told him the wings were not perfect. I had beat into his head the seriousness of the task. As he continued to fall, I had hoped that he would think to flap his arms, but it was obvious that it would do no good. His crutches lacked the resistance to lift his weight against the air. Oh Apollo! I saw my son falling as I'd seen Talos fall, and I knew. I watched as he fell into the tainted sea. And together we cried.

Now, after having returned to the ground several days ago, I sit here collecting my thoughts for the doubters. A huddled mess of emotions, I realize that my days of invention are over. Damn man and his quest for flight; may his every vehicle to the stars melt and break apart. And curse me and my inventive mind that crafted these sticks of hell, curse me that never once turned to check on my son's flight until it was too late. With no purpose left, I will sit here awaiting the mob, the voices, or the gods who will soon take over.

It is my hope that this writing will be sufficient. I will not retell it. Despite the fact that no one saw the bond created in our last days, I assure you it is true. I had no malice toward my son. In fact, in his last days I gave him the greatest thing he had never had: a name. At least they will remember his name. Icarus.

16. THE WHITE SHADOW AND THE DRAGON THAT WASN'T
by David Perlmutter

Clutching the handle of the knife that was carefully concealed upon her person, Jamey stalked with stony determination through the fairytale landscape in which she had found herself. Her blonde hair cut short into a pageboy style, and her glimmering albino skin and foot soldier's garb covering a powerful body beneath, she stalked forward in the name of achieving her goal.

Even among a world full of magical beings—elves, dwarves, fairies, witches, wizards, dragons and the like—Jamey was a figure of incalculable threat and menace. Being as she was one of the few non-magical human beings who had ever stumbled into this realm, and—through her immense physical strength, speed and cunning—shown herself to be a mistress of danger in combating any threat thrown her way, her name was already well known in the plains and corridors of the land. However, as she happened to be an efficient and cold-blooded killer and thief besides, this added considerable infamy to her reputation when she faced the residents of her new home. Especially if her intent was to murder them in the name of achieving the many solid gold coins that would come her way if the job was completed satisfactorily.

Jamey, who was thirteen years old by Earthly standards, nevertheless was treated as an equal—and superior—to all in that world, where age was not an issue since time was not kept there. Her knife cut deep and sharp into anyone whom she was assigned to kill—and sometimes into those who betrayed her or refused to pay her the coins she was owed for her tasks. And, since Jamey was a scoundrel through and through—she'd been a delinquent in her old home and had not changed much since her arrival in the magical realm—she tended to drink and make merry with great glee after her kills, with the result that she inevitably needed to make yet another kill in order to set herself right with her debtors. She did not relish her task of killing so many so often, but, as she had few other options to earn the coins she needed in this universe, she had to do it—or else she herself would become hunted, rather than hunter.

The task now on her plate seemed considerably onerous to her. A purple dragon had supposedly been terrorizing the countryside, and several of Jamey's regular clients had collaborated to provide her with a sum considerably higher than her usual salary to bring the beast in. The price was something she dared not refuse.

However, it seemed like it would be over sooner than she thought. Right after she left town, she spotted the very dragon she was supposed to kill—right in front of her!

"Prepare to die, scaled fool!" Jamey bellowed. "I know well of you and your misdeeds, and it is my sworn duty to punish you for them. Now!"

She unsheathed her knife from her pants and rushed at it, bellowing incoherently but still with angry intent.

Then, to her surprise, it spoke to her:

"Wait!"

Jamey stopped in her tracks. The dragon's voice was as feminine as her own, perhaps even more so, since she displayed a fear uncommon to Jamey but much more common in the weak-bodied gadabouts girls of her age.

What manner of sorcery is this?, the girl warrior spoke to herself. She was familiar with all the means of sorcery known to that world, and had defeated those who had tried to stop her with it before. Yet she had never encountered a speaking dragon before. Like many in her world, she thought of dragons in purely uncomplimentary terms, and any human traits, such as speech, were things she believed they were simply not capable of.

She determined to find the truth behind this enchantment before it meant her end. Preserving her survival had always been her only concern in her short life.

"Did you address me, beast?" she demanded.

"I did," the dragon said, answering Jamey's female assertiveness with her own. "And there's no need for calling me that."

"Calling you what, demon?" retorted Jamey, as she palmed her sharp blade. Her patience was wearing thin, but so was the dragon's.

"Again, no need for the insults. I'm just trying to...."

"I may address my prey in however a fashion I wish—*if* I wish to address them at all, and *if* they are capable of addressing me lucidly. Which a scaly helion such as yourself is not entitled to do!"

That pushed the dragon over the edge. It—or rather, she—let loose a fierce jet of flame from its mouth, one which Jamey, even with her athletic speed, had difficulty escaping without being burned.

"How dare you!" the dragon stormed. "Have you any idea what I've been through today? God! I get ripped out of my world—the only one I've ever known, thank you—and get transported to this weird place I don't know, and get stuck here without any conceivable way of getting back, and now I get dealt with like I'm the one who did something wrong. You need to learn how to address other people in a friendlier way, or else...."

"Silence!"

During the dragon's tirade, Jamey had marched up towards her as planned, and, with the command, was now holding the dragon's long throat with her right hand, while preparing to stab it violently with the knife held in her left.

"I will tolerate no more insolent words from your blasphemous lips, creature of hell!" the warrior stormed. "I have been paid—and handsomely, at that—to eliminate a foul beast befitting your description that profanes our lands at this moment. And, by God, that is what I intend to do!"

"But you cannot!" the dragon protested.

"And why not?"

"Because I am not a real dragon!"

"Not a real..." Jamey lessened her grip on the dragon's throat, and temporarily dropped her knife as the implication of what was being said hit home. Temporarily, for she quickly picked it up again.

"Liar!" she snarled. "You have the body, the scales, the fangs, and indeed, the very fire of a dragon. And yet you claim to be a false creature to deceive me! See how false you consider this!"

She took a swipe at the dragon's head, but the dragon ducked. Not only that, she decided to get tough.

"You bitch!" she snarled. "I need help, not abuse!"

"You will get none from me," Jamey declared passionately.

"Then I might as well get rid of you, then!" answered the dragon.

She breathed fire at Jamey, who ducked again, and then lashed Jamey with her tail, which knocked her to the ground and caused a smear of blood to flow down from a wound on the side of her head. Livid, Jamey leapt to her feet and sprang upon the dragon, pulling her to the ground by the throat. Dragon and girl became entwined as they continued to curse, swear, and fight with each other. Unable to control their momentum, they fell down a hillside in a tightly constructed ball and crash landed into a tree at the bottom of the hill.

The dragon was hardly winded, and intended to destroy Jamey once she righted herself, but the girl, physically weakened by the battle, now supplicated herself before the dragon with what strength she had left.

"Hold, dragon!" Jamey said. "I yield. Your power is too great for me. Do with me what you will, and be merciful, as I was with you."

"Merciful?" The dragon was sarcastic in tone. "Trying to kill me is merciful? You are lucky I don't burn you alive! Especially considering I would never have allowed anyone to lay a hand on me in my old life. That would have meant their death, instantly."

"Of what do you speak?" Jamey inquired.

"Do you not understand our customs? A Princess should not be harmed, for our lives are too valuable to ourselves, our guardians, and protectors to be wasted in such a fashion. At least, mine was until now."

Immediately upon hearing the "P" word, Jamey's whole attitude toward the dragon changed. Again, she assumed the supplicant position, hoping to avoid any burning royal wrath.

"Forgive me, my liege!" she said as tears formed in her eyes. "I am merely a poor huntress, attempting to maintain a living for myself in this hostile environment, and I had no idea to whom I spoke. Please spare me if you are so inclined...."

"Save your breath!" interrupted the dragon/princess caustically. "I am not a Princess of this realm, so your fealty is wasted on me. I have been cruelly exiled from my own realm, and I have no idea how I am to return." Tears now began to form in *her* eyes, and, unlike those in Jamey's, they began to fall to the ground.

"You are a victim of sorcery, I presume?" Jamey asked, getting to her feet.

"Precisely," the dragon responded. "A usurper conspired to deprive me of my throne. She wished to do so not with physical force, but with magic. Without my knowing, I was enchanted by some far away force, and driven away in spite of my protests of innocence, for there, unlike here, dragons are not welcome."

"I know of what you speak," said Jamey. "I, too, was exiled from my home. Persons of my race, the White Shadows, were unwelcome there. I am the last one, and circumstances forced me here, in dire straits. Hence my current position. You must forgive me for my impudence, Princess."

"If you will forgive mine, White Shadow, I believe we may reach an understanding."

"Then I will."

Jamey, once the dragon hater, patted the fearsome beast as if it were a dog, and the dragon allowed her to do so without breathing further flame. Evidently, a friendship was beginning.

"Have you any idea of the name of the usurper who enchanted you?" Jamey said as she embraced the dragon.

"There is none who could have done so with such calculated and effective resolve," said the Princess, "other than Cugel the Magnificent. That mage is so powerful, it is said that he is able to transport himself and others across realms vast and far, not unlike what happened with me—"

"Cugel!" interrupted Jamey.

"I take it you know of him?" said the dragon.

"Know of him? It was that fool himself, and none other, who commissioned me to kill you! For he lives in this very land! And now I know why he was so eager to have me accomplish this goal—for he had something to gain from it!"

"What?" roared the dragon.

"Indeed!" declared Jamey. "Though I thought him old and feeble, as he seems to never leave the nearby tavern in which I always seem to encounter him."

"Tell me in what direction this tavern is!" demanded the dragon/princess. "I will destroy him for what he has done to me."

She very well may have gone on the fiery rampage she was planning, but Jamey stopped her by crying out "Hold!"

"Have you any objections to my idea?" the dragon glowered.

102

"None," said Jamey. "I despise the old fool, and wish to see him destroyed myself. But you want to be made normal and returned to your realm, do you not?"

"Yes."

"Then how will you become human again and return to your realm if he, who is the only one who can accomplish this, is destroyed?"

This made the dragon pause.

"Aah!" she uttered. "I can clearly feel my humanity drain from me as the moments pass, Shadow. I cannot think of anything to do save brute force. Have you any idea of how we may better accomplish our goals, you with your still human brain?"

"I do," said Jamey. "And I shall tell you of my idea now."

The tavern was crowded, and, as usual, Cugel the Magnificent was at the center of it, fully lubricated with ale. It was going full and well and lively, when a voice cried out vengefully:

"Cugel!"

Jamey entered the room. Her reputation preceded her, and so all of the rough and tumble men and magical beings made room for her to encounter the decrepit wizard, who, since alcohol had only a limited effect on him, was still formidable.

"What makes you confront me so, White Shadow?" he declared.

"You should know, old man!" she said, drawing her knife out. "It was your doing!"

"Of what do you speak?"

"I speak of how you dared to imprison a Princess in the body of a dragon, and then allowed me to risk my life in your service to kill it, not knowing her true origins!"

The wizard got to his feet.

"Who told you of this?" he demanded. The anger in his voice rose, and, if he were pushed, he would surely destroy her for being so impudent to him. Yet Jamey knew this already, and she, with her quick mind, was prepared for any actions he might take.

"It was she herself!" declared Jamey.

"What?" He had probably not been expecting this, and was taken off-guard.

Just like Jamey wanted.

"You are well versed in the art of transformation, Cugel," said

Jamey. "Yet you did not destroy the essence of her humanity in doing so. She retains her thoughts, her memories, and her feelings of what happened to her, and she has told me that it was you who exiled her to this land. And she is here with us now as I speak!"

At these words, as if on cue, the straw roof of the tavern burned to a crisp. Mindful of the flame, a giant, clawed appendage pushed the burning straw away, revealing the presence of the princess-cum-dragon. Reacting to her fearsome presence, the tavern patrons scattered in panic. Cugel might well have done so himself, but Jamey grabbed his tunic, pulled him towards her, and struck her knife to his throat.

"Unhand me," he pleaded. "It will destroy us," he added, indicating the dragon fearfully.

"I should murder you for what you did, old man," said Jamey, hatefully. "Or, better yet, have her do it. But I will be as merciful as she was with me. I will spare you your life, if you agree to reverse the evil spell with which you enchanted her, and have her returned to her realm unharmed. Otherwise, you will die at my hand—now!"

Cugel knew it was an offer he could not refuse, so he nodded in agreement, and Jamey dropped him to the ground.

He first undid the spell that had transformed the Princess into the dragon, turning her back into the purple-clad, dark-haired girl she had once been. But, before she was transported back to her realm, the Princess insisted on a caveat.

"I wish to have the Shadow accompany me," she pronounced. "She has proven her worth and loyalty to me, and I could not ask for a more loyal servant. From now on, I wish her to be my military advisor and bodyguard—if she agrees."

"I do," said Jamey. This was the kind of break she had wanted all of her life.

"That cheers me," said the Princess. "I plan to revenge myself on those who exiled me, and I shall need a soldier of excellent caliber to assist me."

"I assure you I will be of such caliber," said Jamey.

And, given her soon-to-be long and successful reign as the personal bodyguard and military commander of the most feared and destructive Princess that realm had ever known, she surely was.

17. THE TIME MERCHANT
by Tim Tobin

"Mr. Miller, you look like a man who can afford ten dollars," said Annie.

"I suppose," replied Harry.

"Tell you what," she continued. "I'll sell you ten minutes for ten dollars. You can spend the ten minutes any way you want. All at once, one minute at a time. However you like."

"Impossible," countered Harry.

"No," said Annie. "Magic."

Every afternoon, Harry Miller stared at the office clock from his cubicle. At exactly 5:00, he logged off his computer, grabbed his jacket, and ran down the three flights of steps two at a time. The 5:13 train home might leave without him if he took time to wait for the elevator.

A book store, a dry cleaner, a hamburger joint, and other store fronts on his two block jog to the train station blurred as he hustled past them. He arrived out-of-breath at the station at precisely 5:12, just in time to jump aboard the train and grab his usual seat.

He caught the local train at 5:46 on the rare occasions that he missed the 5:13 express. That train made every stop and wasted much of Harry's precious time in the evenings, and by the time he got home, Janice had already thrown dinner on the table and yelled at the twins.

So Harry always sprinted to the station to make the earlier train.

In his daily rush, he missed an "opening soon" sign on a new store. Even though fresh paint adorned the store inside and out, the windows sparkled, and trucks unloaded merchandise. Harry ignored the new store. He even ignored a bright red-on-blue sign proclaiming the store to be "The Time Merchant."

Getting home to Janice and the children on the 5:13 consumed all of his energy.

A few days after The Time Merchant opened, Harry did take notice, but only because a beautiful young woman was outside washing the windows. Red hair the color of flames ran down her back in curls. She glanced at Harry with emerald green eyes and a pert nose dotted with freckles.

Harry stumbled over his own feet and fell flat on his face in front of the young woman.

"Oh, my!" she exclaimed. "Sir, are you hurt?"

"No, no. I'm fine," stammered Harry. "Gotta go."

Annie O'Malley stood with her hands on her hips and watched Harry run down the block and then turn into the train station.

"Well, well, Mr. Miller," she said to herself. "Nice to meet you!"

The next day, Harry paused for a moment at the store window, where an array of beautiful watches gleamed in the afternoon sun. Then Harry hurried past the store with just a glance at the closed door.

A week later, Harry called Janice and told her the boss needed him to work overtime and to expect him home on the local. Harry put down the telephone as his wife told him what she thought of the idea. Harry wanted, needed, to see the woman at The Time Merchant again.

Modern and antique timepieces greeted Harry as he entered the shop, and the window display held wristwatches from cheap digital watches to the most expensive luxury watches available. The size of the store had deceived Harry from the outside. The inside of the shop held grandfather and grandmother clocks, and dozens of antique cuckoo clocks filled one wall. The shelves attached to the other wall displayed pieces from modern quartz to ancient sun dials.

The shelves standing against the back wall held books on making and repairing clocks, the history of time keeping, and Stephen Hawking's books on the physics and philosophy of time, along with volumes on the mythology of time in cultures around the world. Right in the middle of the store stood a crystal ball that rested on a solid gold clock. The sparkling ball seemed free of imperfections, and mythological fairies and elves adorned the golden clock.

Surrounded by a world of time, Harry lost track of his own. He became so engrossed in exploring the store that he forgot to look for the young woman who worked there, and when a soft voice spoke to him, he tripped over his feet again.

"Welcome to The Time Merchant, Mr. Miller. My name is Annie O'Malley, and I own the shop."

Annie took so long to show him the many treasures that her shop held, Harry missed the 5:46 local. The next train was an express at 6:13. He took a moment and called Janice to explain that his assignment had taken longer than expected, and she hissed at him to take his damn time.

Annie sympathized with Harry. But when she offered to sell him ten minutes for ten dollars, Harry out and out did not believe her, especially when Annie told him she worked magic.

"So, you're a witch?" asked Harry with a chuckle in his voice.

"I've been called that," replied Annie. "But I don't wear black or ride a broom," she added with a laugh.

Annie stroked the crystal ball, and every shade of the rainbow danced through its interior.

Harry stared at the ball, unimpressed.

"Not much of a trick, Annie," he told her.

An instant later the ball cleared again.

"Very well, Mr. Miller," she huffed. "You now have my gift of ten minutes."

Annie disappeared into a back room and locked the door. Harry's watch read 6:12, and his race to the station took almost ten minutes, so he ran hoping the train was behind schedule.

Passengers still streamed onto the train as Harry arrived on the run. Harry jumped aboard just as the train began to move, and he checked his watch after he found a seat. When he craned his neck to see the station clock as the train pulled away both timepieces read 6:13.

The ten minute run from the clock shop had taken exactly one minute.

Janice Miller hated being a nag. She loved her husband and respected how hard he worked, but her entire world turned upside down if Harry was not on time. They sat down to a late dinner; Harry spent less time with the cranky twins, who stayed up too late.

Arguments always ruined the little time Janice and Harry spent together. And regardless of what time her evening ended, the next day started when the four-year old girls woke up raring to go. Janice started out every day already exhausted.

She worked as a medical assistant in a doctor's office, and like Harry, she watched the clock. But unlike Harry, if the doctor needed her after hours, she stayed. When that happened, Janice needed Harry at home.

Janice's constant harping about time affected their marriage. Distrust crept into her routine, and Harry confirmed her suspicions when he started making excuses about working.

Harry began to visit the beautiful witch every day. Somehow Annie worked her magic, and no time passed when they were together. For a while, Harry lived in the best of his two worlds.

Janice rejoiced at Harry's punctuality, and the twins delighted their father every night. But best of all, Annie's magic made time for them to be together.

They spent uncounted hours talking. He told her of his troubled marriage, about the joys of coming home to the girls, and he told her about the time he didn't have.

In turn, she told him about her home in Ireland, about how she had learned the secrets of witchcraft from an old hag centuries earlier. Harry learned that Annie prowled the globe looking for people like him, for people who always needed more time.

One afternoon, he invited her for a cup of coffee. As he opened the door of The Time Merchant for her, their hands touched. Neither of them let go. From that moment on, their futures, their destinies, were intertwined.

Harry fell in love with Annie.

They stood on an emerald green plain—the same color that sparkled in Annie's eyes. A single elm tree cast a gentle shadow over a bed of rose petals. Harry watched in wonder as hundreds of rainbow colored dots of light flitted through the branches of the trees, and he looked to Annie.

"Fairies," she explained. "Harry, we are in a land of enchantment: Old Ireland, my home."

Annie took Harry's hand, and they lay together on the pink rose petals. They shaded their eyes to watch an azure sky. Only a drifting powder puff cloud broke the blue.

Annie turned and reached for Harry.

They made love that afternoon on a bed of rose petals under an elm tree in ancient Ireland.

Afterward they lay together, bodies touching gently. A slight movement on the plain caught Harry's eye, and he sat up to see better. A very small man pushed a wheelbarrow and picked the occasional daffodil that dotted the vast green meadow.

Annie chuckled. "An elf, Harry. Ireland has many."

"An elf? Of course," mumbled Harry.

He lay back down and reached for Annie. She came softly to him.

Spent, Harry watched songbirds soar across the blue sky and fly onto the tree. The birds serenaded the lovers with a sweet but sad tune, and a slight nagging tugged at Harry's brain. He glanced at his watch, surprised to see that no time had passed since he and Annie had stepped into this magical place.

The nagging became guilt as Harry thought of Janice and his children. He stood and paced around the tree until Annie stood too and took his hand. They walked together in silence, while the blue sky turned grey and storm clouds replaced the white powder puffs. A stiff breeze rattled the branches of the trees, and hundreds of fairies fled for safety. A gentle rain began to fall and then became a torrential downpour. Harry grasped Annie as thunder rolled across the plain.

Lightning lit the horizon and moved their way before a brilliant white bolt of lightning split the elm tree in half. At that, Annie led Harry to the tree, and they stepped into the smoldering trunk. Within an instant, they were safe and dry back in The Time Merchant.

Harry's watch ticked again, but only a few seconds had passed.

Harry looked around for Annie, who had disappeared into the back room. Harry sighed and, racked with guilt, stepped onto a rainy sidewalk and made his way to the train and home.

The next day, Harry stopped at The Time Merchant, but found the store empty. Dirt and grime covered the windows and the sign and rust claimed the wrought iron hand rail. A sturdy lock kept Harry out.

Harry found an envelope taped to the door with a note addressed to him.

"Dearest Harry," it read. "My fate is to help those like you. And my gift to you is all the time you will ever need. And, Harry, I do love you."

Annie had signed the note in her delicate handwriting.

Harry's head whirled, and he almost fell. He stumbled onto the steps of The Time Merchant and closed his eyes, and a vision of the green plain filled his mind. The elm tree stood there, intact, and a path led away from the tree. His mind followed the path to a small village full of quaint cottages where he saw Janice chatting with an elf pushing a wheelbarrow full of flowers. His two children giggled, ran, and played nearby.

Annie had given them a life in a place where time no longer mattered.

And she had given Harry a life with enough time for whatever he wanted.

Harry worked long hours. He strolled to the train and shopped in stores he had never seen before. He went to movies and plays and even took tennis lessons. But a dark and lonely house met him when he arrived home.

His girls, his joys, were gone. No children ran and jumped into his arm yelling "Daddy!"

Harry even missed Janice, the nag. His conscience ate at his soul, while his heart ached for the twins. He wanted his family, his wife and his children, back.

Only Annie could make this right, so Harry began the search. For months, Harry combed the Internet for Annie O'Malley. He found her across the country in Los Angeles, where an announcement for a new business proclaimed the opening of The Time Merchant. He searched for a phone number; he wrote to the address given in the announcement but got no response.

Over the next year, Harry watched Annie open stores all over California. Some were open for a few weeks, and others for only a few days. He then he watched her move north towards Seattle and eastward through Minneapolis and Chicago towards Boston.

Only a few hundred miles more! Annie was returning! Harry's heart soared.

Each day Harry passed the abandoned store hoping for a glimpse of Annie. One day, as he looked for signs of life, he noticed the door ajar. He rushed up the steps, pushed the door open, stood in the gloom of the once magnificent shop, and hoped.

The faint glow of Annie's crystal ball emerged from the dark, and the lovely Time Witch stood behind the globe. Harry wanted to rush into her arms, but she ran away from him, so he put out his hand and waited.

Annie slowly walked toward him. When they were about a yard apart, Annie extended her hand and they melted into each other.

"Oh, Annie," Harry whispered.

"I missed you so," Annie breathed into his neck, but then she gently but firmly pushed him back a foot.

"I know you can't use your gift. You miss them too much."

Harry grew very quiet. His heart needed Annie, but the loss of his family had cost him far too much.

A tear slowly made its way down Annie's cheek.

"Harry," she whispered, "perhaps I can still fix your problem."

She led him to the darkness in the back of the store. Her crystal ball whirled with light, and she caressed the sphere. The ball cleared to show an idyllic scene of the small village in early Ireland, where Harry saw Janice and the children in the yard of one of the cottages.

The two lovers held each other for a long time. Harry finally nodded, and in an instant, he stood under their elm tree on a bed of rose petals. He stood there for a long moment, but then his eyes searched out the village in the distance.

He strode down the path and across the green plain towards a new home where time stood still.

As Harry drew close, his twins recognized him and came running. "Daddy!"

Annie stood under their elm tree and watched Harry with a mist in her eyes. How could even a witch know she would fall in love with a married man? Once he saw two four-year–old girls squeal with delight at the sight of their father, she turned her back and faced her own destiny.

An unusual sensation came over Annie.

She was late for her next assignment.

18. CAT GOT YOUR TONGUE
by Katherine Sanger

Hazel didn't like Laverne. It wasn't that she really hated her—honestly, she had no strong feelings toward her whatsoever. But Mephie, Hazel's cat, kept making her invite Laverne over. So she did. Truth be told, Hazel was just a little bit afraid of Mephie.

Hazel laid the outdated biscuits on the tray and poured the weak, lukewarm tea into the pot. She'd tell Laverne that she'd run out of milk. Maybe that would stop her from visiting so regularly. But for now, it was too late. The doorbell would ring any second—Laverne was always prompt—and the dance would begin. How to entertain a guest you didn't want to entertain? And how to avoid accidentally mentioning the whole Mephie-made-me-call-you thing?

Hazel had no urge to be locked up in an old folks' home or a mental institution, and she figured it would be one of those two options if she ever slipped up and mentioned that her cat talked to her.

So the doorbell rang, as she knew it would, and she answered it.

"Laverne, how lovely to see you again!"

"Oh, it was just so nice of you to invite me," Laverne said. "I always do so look forward to our tea and biscuits."

They walked to the table and sat across from each other.

"Tea?" Hazel asked Laverne.

"Yes—yes, please. And extra milk, of course."

"I'm so sorry, but I seem to be out of milk. Whoops." Hazel smiled sweetly.

"No—no milk?"

112

Hazel shook her head, the smile still plastered to her face. "I just noticed it this morning, and I didn't have time to make it to the shop."

"But—but—I understand."

Hazel's smile became sweeter. Laverne looked quite put out. Maybe this would be her last visit after all. No more fake friendship. Hazel poured the tea for both of them and offered Laverne the biscuits. Laverne took one and put it on her plate. The silence lengthened, became awkward. Hazel refused to speak first.

Mephie wandered into the room, his tail ramrod straight, his tiger stripes shining and silky. If she hadn't been so afraid of him, Hazel would have admitted that he was a very beautiful cat. He went straight for Laverne, though, ignoring Hazel like she wasn't even there, and began rubbing against Laverne's leg and purse.

"Oh, what a sweet kitty you have, Hazel. Your Mephie is such a charmer."

"Hmmm, yes." She kept her eyes above the table, refusing to look down and acknowledge what Mephie was doing.

Laverne loved on Mephie for a little while, but apparently the lack of milk and the stale biscuits was the deal breaker, because after only half an hour, Laverne took her leave, asking to be excused as she felt she was coming down with a cold. Hazel smiled to herself, but said she hoped that Laverne wouldn't be out of commission for long. Those colds were nasty things, after all.

The door had barely closed on Laverne when Hazel heard Mephie giving orders again.

"Friday? But it's Tuesday now!"

Mephie had never demanded two visits in one week. Was this punishment?

"I got you your favorite tuna from the store," she told him, getting it down from the cupboard and putting it in his bowl. "Look, isn't that yummy?"

Mephie marched to his bowl and looked into it with disdain.

"Yes, yes," Hazel said, hanging her head in defeat. "I'll call her now." She would use the lack of milk as an excuse for call. She'd apologize, pretend she was really interested in seeing her again.

Mephie watched her make the call.

On Friday, Hazel packed her crafting bag with the latest afghan she was working on. She hoped that the sheer level of rudeness would encourage Laverne to stop letting her come over. And maybe Laverne would even stop accepting her calls! It was worth a try.

But Laverne just opened the door, invited her in, and served her tea and biscuits.

Hazel took out her crochet and, ignoring Laverne, got to work on it. Bubbee—Laverne's cat—wandered in and began rubbing on Hazel's leg and bag.

"Oh, your Bubbee is such a sweet cat!" Hazel scratched behind Bubbee's ears in a way she never could do to Mephie. Not that Mephie wouldn't let her—he wanted her to—but it just made her so uncomfortable. It felt too…intimate. Like being married all over again. No, it just felt wrong.

Bubbee got his fill and wandered off to sit in the corner, watching them. Hazel kept crocheting, waiting for something to give, something to break. It had to. It just had to! Then—

"I—I—I don't want you here anyway!"

An outburst. From Laverne! Hazel stared at her.

Bubbee turned to look at Laverne, and Laverne turned bright red.

"No—no—no, I didn't mean that! I'm sorry! I'm just so very—tired. And—and…"

But in that instant, Hazel saw *something* cross between Laverne and Bubbee. And she couldn't be sure, but it felt like that momentary understanding she felt with Mephie. The fear that had flashed in Laverne's eyes…could it be true?

Hazel had to find out more before she said anything. She couldn't risk being seen as the crazy cat lady.

"Laverne, I've been thinking. Why don't we meet somewhere else next time, for tea? I really feel so bad about not having that milk on Tuesday. Why don't I go ahead and take you out?"

"Yes! That sounds lovely." Laverne paused, cocked her head a bit. "But—but only the once, right? Like a special treat. We couldn't possibly afford to go out more than once."

"Oh, you're right about that. In fact, I know just the place. There's that little Italian café, right past the shops on High Street? It's probably far fancier than we need, but just this once. Just to make up for the milk. And cement our friendship."

"De—definitely. Just this once."

114

***

"My—my this place is lovely," Laverne said, picking at the linen tablecloth. "It—it's far nicer inside than out, isn't it?"

Hazel nodded. "Yes, very lovely," she echoed. "Lovely."

Conversation stopped. Hazel really had nothing to say to Laverne. She knew what she had hoped to discover while they were out, but she didn't know how to go about finding it.

They read the menus, made polite chatter about the options. Risotto sounded so foreign, they agreed. Much more romantic than simple rice. They placed their orders, and sat, waiting.

Hazel took the plunge.

"So how is Bubbee doing? My Mephie, he's kind of, well, evil. Really. He, well, he…it's almost like he's human. Like I can understand what he's trying to say." There, she couldn't be any more clear than that.

Laverne bit her lip. Paused. "Yes—yes, my Bubbee is like that, too. Almost like he can communicate with me. Tell me what he wants."

Laverne went back to stirring the sugar in her tea. Hazel watched her, waiting for something else. Another hint. A sign that they weren't just crazy old cat ladies who were imaging things.

Nothing.

The waitress brought their meals, set them down in front of them. Laverne reached for the salt, and Hazel felt the moment slipping away.

"I think my cat is making me invite you over!"

The waitress just nodded, asked if there was anything else she could bring them, and then left quickly, before they could answer.

Laverne was staring at Hazel. "But—but I thought I was the only one!"

They stared at each other, suddenly soul mates and friends. Mephie and Bubbee would be thrilled. Except…

"What—what can we do about it?" Laverne asked. "I—I never thought there was anything to be done."

"Well," Hazel pursed her lips and thought. She'd tried to get rid of Mephie before. She'd even gone so far as to try to coax him into a carrier so she could drop him off at the animal rescue. But it hadn't worked. Her brain always argued that they'd know why she'd done it.

They'd force her to take a test. Put her away for the rest of her life. And freedom—even freedom with Mephie—was better than that.

"I—I think maybe Bubbee has been convincing me that I couldn't get rid of him."

"I think Mephie may have been doing the same thing." Hazel took a sip of her tea, poked a bit at her risotto. "Why are we thinking so clearly now? Why didn't I realize that before?" She asked herself almost as much as she asked Laverne. Laverne slowly shook her head.

"We—we just have to leave."

"What?" Hazel knew she hadn't heard right.

"If—if they can…control us, I suppose, then I don't think we ought to go back to them. We —we just need to leave. R—run."

"Now that's just silly. How can we do that? Just abandon our houses? Go live in council flats? My mortgage is paid off. I'm not going to leave it for squatters!"

"But—but would you rather live with Mephie?"

Hazel sipped some more of her tea. "I can bank with that new Internet thing. And I've always wanted to travel."

Laverne's eyes shone.

They left their risotto and tea to get cold and hailed a cab for Heathrow.

Hazel's granddaughter got the call two weeks later. "Oh my god, Grandma? Where have you been? You want me to do what?"

She went to the house that afternoon. As she opened the door, a stench hit her. Grandma's cat! Had she left it?

He was still there. Thin, but okay. The house was destroyed, though. The kitty must have gotten hungry. And upset.

"Awww, little Mephie! You poor thing!" She picked him up and cuddled him. Then moved him out to arm's length. She didn't like cats. Normally. But this one…he was cute. He was sweet. Something in her wanted to take care of him for the rest of his life.

She called her girlfriend and broke up with her by way of a message on the answering machine. She would live with Mephie from now on.

Maybe she should go call on Laverne's grandson. Just in case he needed any help over there. She should definitely go pay him a visit.

19. KWOTH'S ROPE
by Frances Carden

Based on a legend of the Neur people of South Sudan.

The long grasses shimmer golden tendrils in the eddying heat, and Machar cranes his neck staring upward at the gently swaying silver rope that paints circles in the dust of the village and ascends into the bowing blue of the sky. The scurrying figures who congregate at the bottom take turns climbing steadily, like *sifau* marching in a hungry column through the jungle. It is the season of rebirth again.

Machar frowns. The wrinkles chase each other across his pitted face. His faded leopard skin, which marks him as the village chief, is tied in a frazzled knot across his bony shoulders. He stares at the rope, and she does not come down it. She won't. Not for a long time. Maybe never. His anger grows with age. He gets up, his skeletal body collapsing into itself, a curved question mark, and his bare feet tread down the grass and head toward the savannah and his hut at the edge of a gnarled outcropping of trees far away from the village. Even there he will see the sky rope and the figures, always climbing up, rarely ever coming down anymore. He begged her not to go, not to return for her youth.

The world tilts in mirage colors around him, and the sun climbs the blinding blue staircase of the sky. He walks onward, grateful that his failing hearing dims the chatter of the milling women with all their beads clacking together and the skins of their skirts rubbing as their bare feet churn the dust and their hands longingly caress the rope, waiting their turn to climb into the sky. Her voice is not among

117

theirs, but he can easily hear the shrill, lilting tones as though she is there, her voice echoing across the savannah and laughing at him in each crackling chortle of the grass and glare of the few shaking trees around his hut. The excitement of ascension, the instant community of rope lust. Machar's mouth growls downward, and his jagged white teeth bite into his lip. This is her third ascension. He will never go. He will defy Kwoth to the end. There is nothing good that can come of this constant renewal; his spiraling thoughts of anger are there to chase away the fear that she will never come back. During her last stay in heaven, the grasses browned and dried up, and then the monsoon came and washed the world into swirling puddles three times over before she reappeared. It has been four monsoon seasons since she disappeared the last time in the night, and now it is the season of wind. Still she does not come.

That night, he stares into the vastness of the sky above him, where the moon paints the rope that trails into a speck like that of a glowing star far up in the forever. He looks toward his favorite star, Lipai chiing, the one that looks like a girl. He remembers youth, lying on his back in the grass and pointing to the star, Yaya by his side, before he prayed the rope into the village, and she worshiped it, and everything changed.

The star, he had told Yaya, was like an image of her. It was as though she was painted by moonlight, another version of herself waiting to see the village illuminated by the glowing orb of nighttime seen from above. This was before he got the leopard skin of a chief, before their marriage dance and the lack of children, the binding that could not be bound because without children the ceremony is never finished. This was before old age. Before Kwoth trailed his promises into their young village of old people. Now the girl in the stars is just a symbol of all that is inaccessible, and of all that must change.

Yaya stares down the silver filaments of the rope as it sways in the darkness, each thread glittering in the created light of the suspended moon that catches the embedded jewels used for climbing, gifts to Kwoth that pattern the ascension and sparkle hope into the windy night. The winds in the heavens whip around her, knocking her strings of beads together, clacking the wood gently, just as it swayed and bounced together as she, carrying her husband's treasure in a bundle on her back to buy back her youth again, climbed in the depths of the night and snuck into Kwoth's kingdom. Machar will be happy when she comes down. He will forgive her, as he always does. She sways at the edge of heaven and earth, her legs dangling over the thousands of feet down to her village, which from here does not even exist. She sees only the wide open night, a world devoid of light or landmass below her. She regrets that she cannot climb in the day like the other women, their husbands climbing behind them with bundles of meat from the latest sacrifice of a prized cow, or beautiful beads, or carvings of animals with curved horns and power in their eyes. She regrets the secrecy of night and the hiding of her worship.

She reaches out a hand to stroke the mystical filaments of creation that sing with the sound of exhaling chimes in the tumultuous winds above the dark specked earth beneath her. This rope, this connection between sky and the earth, allows her people to climb up before old age and to restore themselves, the hands of the creator god trailing from the mists of heaven to wipe away the ages and give back the beginnings of all things. It is becoming harder and harder with each climb to return to the earth, to milk the cows in the morning and toil beside Machar as he bends over with age and covers himself with cloth, unlike the other men, to hide what he is becoming.

There are many in the village who are not returning anymore. These past days that merge into months and eventually years—time so meaningless, marked by the passing of a sterile sun—she has sat in the coolness of the heaven realm where the springs are always cold. She has sat among the woman as they work on their beads, their young faces renewed every day. Why keep going back down and aging?, they asked her. Up here, you never grow older, not even by a second. The village returns less frequently to the earth. They prefer Kwoth's realm, where they never see but always feel the god of wind and creation. They enjoy living in this sky garden where the world unfurls below, just over the edge of the smooth platform of the heavenly firmament. Far beneath them is a world of growing older and working that is so distant from them, it ceases to exist, a fading memory. Up here, there is nothing to do but enjoy youth, and courtship, and the bounty of the trees, and a world with no animals and therefore no work. What do the riches of earth mean when they carve marks into your skin and worry lines across your brow? What does the pleasure of owning a large herd of cattle matter when you have to bow your back under the hot sun every day?

Yaya sits on the edge of the two worlds, where the rope spirals down to Machar and the steadily emptying village. She looks up to the stars she longed for in the first youth, and wonders what happened to the man who wanted to live forever, to the man who got his wish when he called on Kwoth, to the man who brought the rope he refuses to climb. It is time that he stopped being chief. Perhaps it is time that she stopped coming to him, but then she remembers his shining face in the sun, building for her the hut among their riches of cattle, and handing her a row of carved beads that still circles around her neck, the only thing not new and renewed. One more time, for his salvation. She starts to climb downward, her feet firm beneath her as she sways between heaven and earth and crawls the course of eternity back to the man of her first, natural youth.

In the season of wind, the sky rope twists circles, the gust sighing through the flashing silver filaments like passionate voices whispering across distance, as it sways in the sleeping center of the village. The rounded mud huts sit in clusters, whips of speckled dust motes writing patterns in the streaks of sunlight, the sun itself hanging like the quivering eye of a sacrificed bull as it opens into the west. Large bovine heads with sharp curved horns, curling out with the fierceness of a god, lower to the sparse grass and look across the awakening savannah, where the durra-birds are courting mischief. Inside the huts, fitful dreamers awake, all except Machar, who will sleep into the thrumming heat of the afternoon. Machar, who is far away from the village in his own hut, built among the riches of his dwindling herd, now isolated, a place no longer of respect but abandon. The villagers do not understand him, and as time passes, the rope calls more and more frequently. The village is disappearing into a different world, where they can sit and nap under large Thou trees and the woman can arrange elaborate headdresses while Kwoth keeps the march of seasons paused and the earth world below grows wild and desolate.

Down the rope a slender figure with the characteristic height and regality of her people, Yaya climbs toward her frail, bent husband, each step transitioning her into the stirring heat of a beginning day, the unaccustomed sweat that she has already forgotten trickling into her eyes. She stops several times and fights the impulse to rush back upward. She can feel the heaviness of life again, the skin settling into the elements, her muscles no longer accustomed to the daily toil straining to make the descent between heaven and earth. She is growing older again already, and she can feel the pain of fear. She has stayed up too long this time, and she slips and slides down the rope several times. The jewel offerings woven into Kwoth's rope cut her palms and decorate the rope in a new kind of sacrifice, the red glittering and absorbing into the silver. Her resolve strengthens. She will never leave the heaven realm again after this. The climb swirls in Yaya's head like the eddying mirage of a nightmare, insubstantial yet inescapable and always transforming. Only her memory of the man and of what their love had once been, back before the rope when they met as she brought water to her father's cows, sustains her in this, her last effort.

Machar remains asleep in his hut, nestled under the leopard skin that marks him as important but only on this one plain and no longer to the people, who only want the rope and youth. His frail body, puckered in on itself like a soured prune, shivers as his dreamless eyes twitch and rove behind his lids, searching for something that he will never find. Asking is such a dangerous thing. The six long, straight cuts engraved into his forehead, the symbol of his transition from a boy to a man, are strong and straight. He was brave, he did not flinch. That was the night he won Yaya, the night when they later lay in the grass under the stars and he knew that the marriage ceremony binding them together would soon begin. Then time was so important, the elapsing of months as each cattle trade was undergone, each ritual met. But now, with the rope, all those things mean nothing. He sleeps on, and the lowing of his cattle, needing milking, does not wake him. Dust from the grassland whips in through his open hut and settles on the molting leopard skin.

Yaya is tired and thirsty, her body no longer accustomed to all the physical exertion. Her proud back bows, her height and beautiful bearing diminishing with the burning in her arms and legs and the seeping cuts carved by all those jewels and even the silver filaments of the rope that stick barbed points into her slippery palms. She falls the last few feet down the rope and lands in a dusty heap at the bottom, where the path is beaten down from so many people coming and going. The skins of her skirt are scarred with her own drying blood and already the flies, who cannot ascend to heaven as the people, begin to cover her with excited twitching of their frantic, thirsty limbs. The nature of this world repels her. If Machar will not return with her, then she will ascend the rope and stay with the beautiful people of the sky, and she won't think of him again.

She crawls to the well in the center of the village, still quite as day opens. She pulls a dangling wooden bucket, which clinks against the side of the well like a giant bead necklace swinging around the neck of a goddess. Finally, it brings her the taste of stagnant earth water, crawling with dust and simmering already in the hot sun. She brings it to her cracked lips, her beauty already diminishing in the reality of a world to which she no longer belongs. She waits as the sun bleeds across the sky under the dimpled shade of the Thou village tree, and then with the setting of the sun, her energy somewhat restored, she begins the walk to Machar's hut. This time, she will make him accept Kwoth. She will make him bring tribute and climb the rope before he withers away like the inexplicable skeletons of the dumb animals who do not have the gratification of climbing heavenward.

Machar sleeps, half sitting, in his hut, the passage of a familiar shadow before his door drawing him out of the escapes of dreams. He stares upward, the setting light behind the figure bright like the sparkling of gold around a woman's neck; the tall figure with an elegant headdress is nothing but a silhouette, the head bent down to look in on him. He is embarrassed to be found sleeping on the matt of his barren hut and squints his eyes, hoping the outline is real and not another joke, not another answered supplication that turns double.

"Yaya?" The word trickles across his tongue like water and with it rises the longing that he hates himself for feeling every time she returns.

The figure does not answer, but merely stays pinned in the doorway, the light falling around it like a metal current, liquid and hard at the same time, a slippery surface that an insect might bang against, frantic wings beating for escape. The longing seeps out as the poison of the moment draws in, and Machar remains sitting. He will not stand. He will not honor the woman who left him.

Yaya, her voice spilling around her with the fluidity of the angry and the tired, accuses him, mocks him for sleeping through the day. Why respect a chief who will not climb the rope? Why honor a chief who remains outcast from the village? Why listen to a chief whose cattle are even now crying from heavy udders and whose backs do not sport the streak of honorary ashes for the cow spirits that have gone before them? Above all, why come back to a frail and broken thing where once a man had been? Had he lost the bravery of the marks, which even now in age are shrinking to puckered white lines that no longer spoke of resilience, but of weakness, of fear. But hadn't she come back for him after all, even though he had given her no children and therefore the marriage was never final, never real? Had she not stayed with him anyway? Had she not supported him? Had she not tolerated his foolishness, mostly because he had, despite himself, brought them the miracle of the rope and the closeness of Kwoth, who rode the air and traveled the sky? But now, look at him, grown weak and frail. He proves in his stubbornness, in his refusal to go to Kwoth, that there is nothing down on this earth to stay for. He is a living testament of what age had to offer. Yaya pauses, the melodic sounds of her language marred by the words she speaks. She gropes for breath as she looks down on this man who had promised to put her up in the stars with Lipai chiing. Instead he purposefully grew weak, a stubborn old fool sunken into himself and lying helpless on the floor of their hut. She had forgotten her anger, even started to miss Machar in the kingdom of the sky, but now that she sees him again, older and more brittle, all that love is replaced with something else that burns bright in her chest.

Machar, in the many monsoons that have passed, however, has grown angry with Yaya, his rage filling and expanding the hollow places left in his chest as he watches the people, at first going up the rope every once and a while, then going up weekly, daily, and finally never coming down again. The village that once rang with dances and the sounds of ceremonial drums now mostly silent, with the few remaining people dreamy eyed, going to the gathering pool every day to stare disconsolately at their shifting images, prodding long fingers along imaginary creases and looking toward the silver rope weaving the sky. He has prepared for this day, hoped with a finality that he could wait until she returned. And now she has. He apologizes to her, reaches out beseeching hands with callous, work-worn palms, and talks of being ready to climb the rope, points frantically to a pile in the corner of the hut of grains and talks of a sacrificed bull, fresh meat to bring to the kingdom in the sky. If only she will rest with him here this one night, they will sacrifice the cow in the morning and he will follow her; she can help him ascend the rope that he is finally ready to climb.

Yaya sighs in relief, her features returning to the familiarity of their first meeting, her smile wide and freshly innocent across her face as she comes into the hut and sinks to her knees, her hands searching for Machar's and shuddering with revulsion as she feels the rough, bony hands against hers. Soon, both of their hands will be restored and the blood, scars, and toil wiped away for the final time. She sees herself sitting forever by the stream with Machar in a land of no work, no worrisome animals, no definitions other than youth and rest.

In this moment, he feels the same stirring as he does each time when Yaya returns, so bright, like she looked on the day he first saw her, tall and nearly floating with an ease of body and nature, strolling among her father's cattle. Each time, he hates himself for this response to his constantly rejuvenated wife, hates the temptation that rises in his own soul and the longing for the rope that he does not trust and the ephemeral sky world that has transformed and taken his people.

That night Yaya stays with him in the hut and her movements, the way she keeps away from him and tries not to look, the disgust over his aging that hangs between them in the air like smoke over water, builds the longing and the hate equally in his chest. He thinks of the carved and sharpened cattle horn, hidden beneath his leopard skin, and he waits, waits for his chance.

The night is full of deepness, the moon shining ovoid in the sky over the waving grassland and through the chittering of rubbing tree leaves, when Machar steals out to the village with the cow horn, long and polished in his shaking palm, covered with a sheen of precise sharpness, the product of his last strength.

He makes his way through the grass stealthily and, for the first time in a long time, wears the significance of his leopard skin, which gives him a ferocity in the nighttime that edges him toward his mission. They say Kwoth created them. They say that he rides the air and the sky, is everything and nothing at the same time. But he feels no presence tonight, and if anything stops him, it will be human. But Yaya is deeply asleep, dreaming of sky realms and faces without wrinkles who proudly bear the scars of manhood and do not shrivel, curled onto a hut floor around the remnants of a powerful chief, alone and unlovable. The thoughts chase him through the night, and by the time he has reached the village and the base of the too-long sky rope that trails several lax inches into the dust, he is breathing hard. His body thrums with the daring nature of his intention. He pictures running toward the rope, his arm raised and the bone catching along the slick surface as it arches downward and in a swift motion severs the silver rope, which he imagines falling and coiling about his feet. He will wear a portion around his neck with his leopard skin, so that everyone will know he is the man who defeated the power of the rope. They will worship him and tend his flocks, and what does it matter if he is old? Only the animals cave into piles of bones, after all.

Yet, as he approaches the rope, the silver and the jewels wink at him in the lulling moonlight. The night is alone and open to just him. He looks down at his once powerful hands, where he clutches the bone blade, but instead of being enthralled by the sharpness of his carving, he is amazed by the frail veins standing along his small hand, by the very shrinkage of himself over time. He pauses to examine himself in the moonlight and wishes the reflecting pool was closer, wishes to see what has happened to his face while all the others climbed the rope. He looks up and follows it into the gnawing darkness and thinks of Yaya, coming back each time as she was— how she never changes, only in that really her personality does change, her pride in him and his cattle, her desire to stay with him even though without children the marriage ceremony will never be complete, never be final, even though he is chief, waning like a flame about to extinguish itself.

He reaches out to the shifting silver filaments and runs a hand along the surface, feels the offerings of jewels and beads woven in, stuck there by all those climbers as they worked their way toward rejuvenation, as their feet steadied themselves on the embedded hopes of others. He thinks of Yaya, all that she has said, and shudders with the horror of what the rope offers, of the fact that on the village's behalf, on Yaya's behalf really, he made the supplication as chief that things would remain the same forever, not really knowing what that meant, not really realizing that there was no formula to continue life as it was or to rejoice in the work and the collections it offered—not when there was the ease of the sky kingdom, the direction connection between heaven and earth that made of his land a weak, undesirable thing.

Suddenly, he wishes desperately for the rope, thinking of those looks of revulsion in Yaya's eyes, of the way that she avoids him as though she doesn't really see him, or at least doesn't want to see him. He reaches out a tentative hand and then a stronger one, drops the bone blade, and grasps the rope to finally climb it, to set out to fulfill the fake promise that offered the only true answer.

But he has let too much time pass. He has grown too old and weak. He cannot climb. The silver filaments serrate his palms but offer no purchase. The jewels and embedded offerings slice at him, but his shaking hands cannot hold on to them long enough to pull himself up, and his frantic struggling simply swings the rope, throws him off into the dirt with a thud that threatens his very bones. He cries out, cries into the night like the song of a hyena, with all the anger and frustration returning in the breeze to mock him.

He flings out his arm, catches up the blade, and rakes it across the still swaying rope as it passes by his form, stranded undignified in the dust that catches in his throat. But the blade only glances off, and his frustration and hurt grows. He catches hold of the rope and saws, pushing his full body weight into the effort, using the last of the strength to cut the tough silver filaments one at a time, continuing to saw as the moon shuts her eye and the sun begins to open its opaque orb over the scene. Finally, the rope snaps in his hand, and he waits for the coil to unravel. Instead, the small length below his curled palm remains and the rest snaps back into the sky, flying up with a singing whirr that wakens the village with a terrified start. Even Yaya far away, who screams as she is torn from her dream of the sky, innately understanding the snapping and the loss of all things.

The remaining villagers emerge, horrified. They find Machar simply sitting with his legs spread around him, the frayed end of the rope clasped in his hand, his leopard skin fallen off and dirty. He stares up at the sky, where the silver filaments snapped and drew up into themselves. From the opposite side of the sky, there is a returned startled cry, and the wailing of the ones above waiting for the ones below, who will never be able to get to them again. Machar looks from one startled face to another, seeing the accusation and hatred growing in the eyes running with tears of loss.

"Bring it back!" they scream. All horrified, they reach to their faces and trace the lines that will start to appear. They grab at their bare sculls, where their shaved heads will someday show a sheen of grey. They pry at their teeth, which will now decay and fall out. They wail and stamp their feet as they look around at the village, fallen into disarray and forgotten, and all that it will demand of them now. They scream and wail and all the time Machar sits with his hand holding the incrimination of his action, his mouth bobbing slightly in the surprise of what he has actually done.

"Bring it back!" they scream. But Machar does not know how, does not know what to say. The words he planned, the rope around his neck glimmering his authority, his leopard skin once more across his shoulders, seem insubstantial now. The horror and anger of his people astonish him, their reaction visceral, their keening mixing with the unreachable sounds from the sky, the quietness of Kwoth, who gives them no more answers.

The monsoon season and the season of the wind comes and leaves many times. The people stare disconsolately at their bodies, which begin to stoop, at the weakness that shuts off their eyes and hearing, at the burning in their frames as they lie down at night and find no rest. Time is once again a marked and hard thing. They stop looking at their images reflected back in the pools and cease to call to the people in the sky, who have long forgotten them. They watch as their chief shrinks into himself more, and as the hollow-eyed Yaya feeds him his ful each night and tends the cattle and his land, her lips never opening again in speech and her eyes always betraying a revulsion and loathing of the man she tends, the scars of long ago bravery hidden by leathery, lined skin. Her scars, along her hands and feet, from the last climb of the rope, however, glow brighter with the passing of time, and when she has a moment, she pauses to stare at them.

They all marvel and congregate around the man, wrapped in his leopard skins, as he chants in delirium. The last frail breath is sucked out of his body with a rattle, followed by nothing. As the time goes on their chief turns to bones; they finger the delicate skeleton and compare it to their own forms. They call to the sky, but Machar is not there, and they finally realize what severing the rope means.

20. TAPROOT HEART
by Carmen Tudor

He followed the lunar cycle as he always had, as his mother and father before him had, and as their mothers and fathers before them had. The way the moon pulled and tugged at the sappy, electro-magnetized veins and inner workings of all green living things—on a microscopic, ethereal plain, he knew—pulled and tugged at him too. He knew that as the new moon rose, so too would he rise from his bed and tend the earth with a love and tenderness that would wane and turn to ash as soon as the phases drew on. By the time the last quarter reached his little patch of earth, his softness would turn to bitterness. His hands would crumble the dirt between fingers, no longer able to caress the lifestuff he was supposed to love.

It was during one such phase that he had looked about him and opened his eyes to a sight at once barren and fertile, green and gray. *What am I doing?* he thought. It came quietly, and he never spoke the words aloud. But somewhere in the back of his mind, they hovered there and threatened to resurface on those cold, dark mornings of the last quarter moon.

So on and on he woke and slept, and turned the soil and, at the right time, harvested what he had sown. What he took from the earth tasted of memories and forgotten oaths. It lingered in his mouth, and as he exhaled after each bite, he wondered if he might breathe some of the bitterness out too. But all bad things, he reasoned, must pass, and after filling him with a depth of sorrow so long as the moon lessened its puppetry, he once again let his spirits rise and comfort him. All that he knew to be his life's work—those little, mundane tasks of turning and tending—was what gave real meaning to his survival. It didn't matter that they were unspoken or unthought of by others; to him, it reamained the essence of existence.

It happened one day that, as he worked, a wind blew heavily from the south and took with it some of his favorite trees. Massive ironbarks and poplars that had been dotted around the old farmstead for longer than he could remember were torn up from the ground. As they flew past the window, he noted how their once deeply planted roots, knotted and gnarled as they were, trailed below them. His gaze fell to the roots, and he smiled at the thought that they were steadfast to the end.

After examining the landscape around him, and taking note of the destruction and devastation to the baby shoots and all the new life so recently cropped up, he dusted off his hands and resolved to begin again. The soil was still rich and willing to feed all those hungry things that opened themselves up in supplication. He bent down low to the ground, and as he trailed his fingertips along the loose soil, he smiled. It was a good week. The moon was waxing bright, and it was an excellent time for lavender and rosemary, and shadowy, tenacious, rooted things.

He planted things he loved, and he planted things nobody ever loved. His mother and father had done so too, and their mothers and fathers before them. To take from the land was one thing, they had always said, but to give back was infinitely better. He chose first a compass. Its brass casing was marred and scarred from many years of ill treatment. Some sailor, he thought, ages and ages ago, must have worn it with pride, but the years of its solitude had not been kind. After rubbing the thing on the sleeve of his shirt, he placed it into the ground and lovingly covered it up. "Goodbye," he said. "And good luck."

Next, he put down an old glove. Where the lonely thing's little friend had disappeared to was a secret he would never learn. Alone, the thing had been discarded. Where he had found it didn't matter. All forgotten, indistinct places are alike, he thought. And all bright, promising places are alike too. He gave the glove down to the earth and covered it up like the first item.

After finishing off the last of his green items—the real plants, the ones that would grow with the certainty of all joyful, living things—

he reached into his basket for the last piece to sow. There in the bottom, pressing its delicate side against the woven reed, was a heart. Like the glove, its other half had abandoned it. Unlike the glove, the heart had no twin. Its string, the part that tethered it to its companion, was severed somewhere in the middle. The man examined it for a moment. *Not cut*, he thought. *Snapped.*

As he held the heart in his hand, he was pleased to find the warm, soft thing beating gently. It would take some time, he knew, to restore it to its former self. With the same care as before, he lowered the little heart to the ground. The rain began to fall softly as he covered it over.

After tying his cravat and combing his hair, the man hitched his wagon and set off for town. He tipped his hat to the ladies he met, and smiled even when they lowered their gazes and pretended not to see. He nodded to the men, and nodded again even when they turned their heads and laughed aloud. He was a proud man, and in spite of his desire to speak his mind, he remembered words his mother and his father, and their mothers and fathers before them, had spoken. *What you take from the world is one thing, but what you give back has the power to change your life...*

He bought grain, he bought blacking, he bought paper and ink. It was his habit of an evening to sit at his window and write the words he couldn't speak. His beliefs and ideals were laughed at by others, but between the moon's rising and setting, the man gave over to an eloquence not yet appreciated in a town of small ideas. One day he hoped to publish a book. Great men and women wrote poetry. It was a sort of music of the heart, he thought; a language spoken not in words, but in emotion and sentiment. It was a language that welcomed defiance and grew stronger because of it. It was steadfast. It was true.

And so he wrote for a while. He thought often. He waited and watched the land.

After tending to his animals and ploughing and even weeding during the full moon, the man watched for the progress of his new perennials—his damson trees, his rosemary, and his lavender. The other things, the little additions of unwanted items, were almost forgotten. Once, during a particularly dark and dismal night, he had scorned his actions. The *What am I doing?* of before was laced with acrimony. He had no answer for himself, and that, he reasoned, was the saddest part of all. In time, however, the sentiment was once again lost to the wind and dropped somewhere and trodden down underfoot. Maybe the greengrocer had it now. Or maybe the gossiping milliner. It didn't matter to him.

The time eventually came again for him to harvest what he had sown. The bright green of the plants, as they opened up to the sun's rays, contrasted prettily against the dark red hues of the rich soil. The wind storm that had carried off the man's beloved trees had, in turn, stirred the soil, and the aeration, he understood, was more than a simple peace offering. Everything he pulled up was shinier than he had seen before. Each strawberry was sweeter than the last. The root vegetables came up with ease and their skins shone in the light. As the man prepared to carry his basket inside, he stopped a moment to glimpse a patch of earth. To the south of the little farmhouse, and directly next to where his favorite poplars had formed an avenue not so very long before, were three new additions to his crop.

The glove, which he had planted with the hope of receiving nothing more than a handful of luck, stretched its fabric-covered fingers skyward.

After taking a step closer, he bent down and wrapped his own fingers around the glove's. He squeezed gently and was surprised to find a firmness there he hadn't anticipated. He pulled the glove up. It resisted at first, as all growing things do, but soon began to slide free from the dirt. The arm attached was covered in a scattering of earth, but the skin below was warm and soft. When the elbow stayed firm, he moved on to the next item.

The compass, as he had left it, wanted little searching for. He soon found strands of dark hair, and as the breeze picked up, it all fanned out and gleamed in the light. Anxious to see what he might unearth, the man continued to dig with his hands. The face that emerged opened its eyes and smiled up. No surprised look crossed her face, but something more, something like amused expectation, formed creases at the edges of the green eyes. "Help me up," she said.

The man moved on to where the heart had been. There, covered in the trailing leaves of what could have been strawberries, was the heart. Its red, tender covering anchored its underside downward. "It's all right," he explained. "I'm trying to help."

The girl nodded. "Oh, I know. But it has a will of its own, you see."

He had made the tool many years earlier. The handle was carved of his own hand. The blade curved sharply in a pointed crescent, and as he dug it into the earth, the girl winced. "Do be careful," she said.

The man nodded. He plunged the blade low enough to encircle the taproot, but not so close as to leave a single mark. After twisting the blade in a full circle, he gently lifted the heart upward. When it was free, he pulled it loose and marveled at the trailing root. The heart beat firmly in his hands. He started for a moment, and then offered his spare hand to the girl, who was finally able to free herself from the field.

She stood upright, and although he was sad to see she had only a single arm, she smiled brightly, and he knew at once she didn't care. He offered her the heart. She took it gingerly and placed in into her chest. "There. All done." She winced a little and then nodded when the heart resumed its normal rhythm.

He took her hand and showed her the animals and the land and the place where the ironbarks had stood. She smiled and told him she knew it all already. She had heard stories whispered to her on the wind of the animals and the uprooted trees and the living, green things that she had been born of. It was funny to be a cast-off, she told him. Funny, but not at all a bad thing.

In return, he told her that he too was a cast-off, but that it didn't matter what the world forgot; it mattered only what we chose to remember.

The girl stayed for several years. In time, her glove frayed and her sense of direction led her out to the field more often than to their home. Her heart, which had always been steadfast, remained so long after the phases of the moon pulled and pushed and reminded her of other places to be.

It was during a wind storm one evening that she rose from her chair. She opened the door, and before the man could look up from his writing, she stepped outside and into the gale. He dashed to the window. There, where his favorite trees had stood a long time ago, the girl raised her gloved hand. The man waved back. She smiled happily and turned, and as the man ran to the door, he thought he heard her voice on the breeze. *It doesn't matter where I'm going; it only matters where I've been.*

The man continued to follow the moon phases long after that time. His mother and father before him, and their mothers and fathers before them, had all done so. It was simple and it was true. It was steadfast, he reminded himself. So much so that each time he glanced up at the waning moon, he thought not of sad things, but only of the impossibly possible girl with the taproot heart. He reminded himself of the trees that had come and gone. He listened to his own written words, the ones that streamed through his mind on quiet, firelit nights. Tomorrow, he told himself, he could begin again.

21. INVISIBLE
by Melody Schreiber

Pat Conley became invisible on a Tuesday.

Well, it may have been a Tuesday. It may have been earlier. How could he know for sure?

He was walking to work as usual when a woman sideswiped him coming out of the Foggy Bottom metro. "Excuse me!" he said, but neither she nor anyone else stopped or even glanced his way.

He walked past the plate glass windows of Starbucks and Subway. He could still see his reflection in the glass, but he made a face and... nothing. No one on the other side of the glass noticed him. He intensified the grimace and then began waving his arms, hooting and hopping. Nothing. Reflected in the glass, his fellow commuters swirled around him on the sidewalk. His antics interrupted no one. A college student chattered on her cell phone. A harried mom pushed her stroller so close his clothes fluttered, but still nothing.

I am invisible, he thought.

He had always suspected this might happen, had felt his edges blurring and fading, but now that he was finally erased from the world, he didn't feel the terror he had expected. Perhaps it had disappeared, too.

Instead, he felt the quick flare of joy.

I am invisible.

I can do whatever I want.

He raised his arms and whooped again. He spun around, careened along the sidewalk like a kid pretending to be an airplane.

"Am I invisible?" he shouted at passersby, because he couldn't quite believe how or when or why it had happened. "Can you even hear me?" he asked, then bellowed, at a young woman in a red dress. Nothing. No looks, just gazes trained carefully ahead.

If you became invisible, what would you do? Would you rob a bank, or sneak into a movie theater, or peek under a lady's dress? Stow away on a plane bound for some far-off destination?

None of those things sounded particularly tempting to Pat Conley. In fact, simply realizing that he was invisible was tiring enough. Pat Conley was a man who valued his routine. Pat Conley found comfort in repetition, in order, in schedules and lunch breaks and update meetings.

And so Pat did just what he wanted: he kept walking to work. After all, even invisible men had to pay their alimony on time. He kept on toward the job he'd devoted his life to, the job he was sure would grant all of his dreams in return for devoting every waking minute to it.

He surely didn't want to return to his empty cavern of an apartment, all stiff white carpet and bare white walls. Six months, and he still hadn't bothered to decorate. He had grown fond of—no, not fond of, *familiar* with—his new ascetic lifestyle. It seemed appropriate for his new life, the blank isolation of this apartment, one of many on his floor, which was one of many floors in a high-rise that itself joined a sea of Alexandria towers. Just another brick in the wall.

Pat Conley's apartment was, in short, the diametrical opposite of the Georgetown branch of PNC Bank. Pat Conley now stood, as he did every day, at the intersection of Wisconsin and M Streets Northwest, across the street from the Georgetown branch, and took in the building as a stranger might.

The first thing visitors notice about the Georgetown branch of PNC Bank is, of course, the gold dome over the entrance. Their eyes move up the pair of grand concrete columns and skim past "PNC Bank" in modest gold letters—the only modest thing about the building. They briefly take in the clock with gold hands and face before moving on to the main attraction: the gilded dome, shining even on the darkest day. Pat Conley's favorite part was just above the dome, however, visible only from across the street: the gold cupola perched proudly against the sky. Nothing Pat Conley had ever seen was freer, bolder, more certain about its place in the world than that gold cupola.

He broke his reverie and hurried across the street. According to the gold-face clock, it was already 8:05 A.M., which meant Pat Conley had reached another unknown milestone: he was late.

Such grandeur outside promised so much more inside, but the inside was always a letdown: air pushed out of lungs, breath drawn a little short. Sure, there were still plenty of features designed to awe: the gold-inlaid marble floor in concentric circles, the dark-wood paneled desks, the vaulted ceilings with intricate trimwork skirting the tops of the walls.

Yet the hushed tomb-like air, the way Pat's heels clicked too loudly upon the floor, the way the security guard examined his cuticles idly: they all combined to weigh upon him as one unit. This was his entire life, and it terrified him each morning. At least he could slip past the guard unnoticed now.

It was always better once he escaped up the stairs to his cubicle. In such a lovely, historic building, there was never enough space. Pat Conley's cubicle was parked between a bathroom and the secretarial pool, where five receptionists filed receipts and took messages for bankers who rarely bothered to show up for work. (Tony, for one, was on a long vacation in the Maldives. Pat knew from Johanna's Facebook photos.) Four of the receptionists chattered constantly—all except for Louisa, who was known by some for "keeping to herself" and by others for "being a stuck-up bitch." When Pat saw Louisa walk by his office to go to the bathroom, he knew the other girls would immediately begin talking about her. In this manner, Pat had learned the difficulties of pulling off a dirndl skirt; the dangers of a messy ponytail; and the downsides of confiding in Jennifer, the loudest receptionist in the pool, who had it on good authority that Louisa was taking Prozac. "I mean, just look at her skin," Jennifer would say. "It totally makes sense."

But Pat wasn't on Louisa's side, not by a long shot. She sat directly on the other side of the wall, and her silence in the office was offset by the reams of complaints she filed against Pat: the way he knocked against the cloth-covered cubicle wall when he rolled back in his chair; the way he sharpened pencils ("almost aggressively," the report claimed); and, worst of all, the constant whistling.

For Pat Conley, whistling was an art form. He didn't whistle any old song that popped into his head; he chose a selection, usually classical music, very carefully, and he put his entire being into whistling it. His chest and lungs often hurt by the end of, say, Wagner's "Ride of the Valkyries."

Louisa had complained about Pat Conley's whistling so much that Jared from HR finally told him, "Sorry, buddy, ya gotta stop." Jared had always been kind to him, in an aimless way, which was more than Pat could say for anyone else in the office. Pat liked to think they would be friends outside of the office, if he could just hit upon the right shared interest. But Pat Conley was, of course, hopeless at football, and he knew next to nothing about grilling a steak or going to a Metallica concert, which he sensed were the types of things Jared did.

On the morning that he became invisible, Pat sat at his desk, careful not to roll back into the cubicle wall, and wondered how many hours would pass before his coworkers discovered he was gone.

By Friday, it was clear that no one missed him. In a fit of daring, Pat forewent his usual bow tie and suit jacket in favor of khaki shorts and the Hawaiian shirt he had bought on his honeymoon. Johanna had always despised it, had called it "the orange abomination," and so the sight of it cheered him up immensely. He'd never seen the appeal of Casual Fridays before now.

Commuting was the worst part of invisibility. A dozen strangers tried to sit in his lap before he gave up and decided to stand on every train and bus. A man of his age, taking the metro! It was shameful. But Johanna had taken the car, along with every other part of his life worth keeping. Occasionally, he lurched into other passengers, or they pushed up against him in a crowded train. Some would look around a little wide-eyed, wondering if they'd felt someone there, but most just kept their eyes glued to their phones and books and newspapers.

Otherwise, Pat Conley had never felt so free.

At work, as he scanned through spreadsheets and accounting programs on his desktop, he began humming. "Pat, my good fellow," he said—for he had begun muttering to himself, now that no one could hear him, and the British accent was a fun bonus—"why hold back?" And so he began whistling. The first song to come to mind was Gershwin's "Rhapsody in Blue." The music soared, delicate yet powerful. It was free, just like him.

He realized, in some distant part of his brain, that Louisa had stood up and left the room next to his, and now he could hear her speaking indistinctly in Jared's office. Her voice rose insistently, and Jared said, "But Lou, he promised to stop." Murmuring. "Oh, OK, fine. I'll talk to him again."

Jared's heavy footsteps made their way down the hall. Louisa, ever the coward, dipped back into her office to resume typing.

Pat sucked in his breath and sat very still in his rolling chair. He knew he was invisible, but still, he wanted to be careful. Jared stuck his head in Pat's office and took a look around. For a second, his eyes seemed to meet Pat's. But no, that wasn't possible. Jared shook his head and walked over to Louisa's desk. "Lou, he ain't even there right now."

A pause. "But, Jared," Lousia finally croaked out. This girl really hated public speaking. "I'm sure I heard something…"

"Maybe he's in the john, I dunno. I'll write this up, though, OK?"

"Can't you check the bathroom?" Louisa asked.

Jared finally seemed to lose his patience. "Check it yourself, if you're so keen on tracking him down," he said. "I'll file your report, but honestly, you shouldn't be so hard on the guy. You know what a tough year he's had."

If he said anything else, Pat didn't hear it. *You know what a tough year he's had.* So Jared pitied him? Did the whole office feel bad for him? *Oh, poor Pat. She left him for his boss, can you imagine? He must be so humiliated.*

He stood up so quickly his chair bumped against the wall, Louisa and her complaints be damned. He strode out of his office, down the stairs, and through the doors, breaking into a run. If anyone could have seen him, they surely would have laughed at the sight: a middle-aged man huffing along the sidewalk in a bright orange shirt. But he was too miserable to feel ridiculous.

He didn't know where he was going until he got there. Pat heaved himself onto the bench in Francis Scott Key Park until his heartbeat slowed again. Far below him, tracing a steady V into the slate-gray river, raced a single crew boat.

He thought about giving himself the day off. Yes, a mental health day! Because being invisible should definitely count as a mental health issue. But what would he do? He was already dreading the long weekend alone in his monk cell of an apartment. Weekends were by far the worst. On weeknights, he could watch enough TV and eat enough Nature's Promise Mac & Cheese to lull his mind into blankness before bed. And in the morning, he was occupied with getting ready and making it to the bus stop and then the metro in time. But on the weekends, he had nothing to occupy him.

Pat Conley stared at the men and women who passed by, oblivious to his watching. He let his mind wander as he imagined what their lives were like. Had they ever woken up to find their whole lives had disappeared?

Being invisible was lonely business. He had thought he might like invisibility, the anonymity of it. But all he wanted was to be seen again. To be acknowledged.

It suddenly hit him, the why. Of course. One doesn't simply become invisible for no reason.

He stood up and began walking toward the Key Bridge, his steps long and purposeful now, his breath coming in confident puffs. The sun was painfully bright, the kind of day where you normally hid behind sunglasses and baseball caps, and when you got back to your cubicle after lunch, you fanned the damp spots under your armpits and said, *Oooh, boy, this weather!* to no one in particular.

But invisible men don't feel the glare, don't sweat. Pat felt cool, even. The sunlight seemed to shine only for him—it illuminated everything he was supposed to do.

He reached the bridge and turned left onto its sidewalk. He paused for a moment, suddenly wondering if he should return to the office to leave some sort of note. But then he shook his head. "For whom?" he asked himself out loud, because he wanted to hear something, anything. "Jared? Louisa? *Tony?*" He laughed, and as he laughed, he climbed over the metal fence.

The sound of the traffic faded. He held on to the fence with both arms spread out to his sides, facing his chest out toward the water like Leonardo DiCaprio. *I'm the king of the world!* He was surprised not to feel any fear, only excitement. Finally, he knew what he was supposed to do. It was strange, though, the way his heart was beating; he could almost make out the whisper of his own name. *Pat. Pat. Pat.*

He closed his eyes and felt his fingers begin to loosen.

Louisa began to scream even louder.

"Pat! Pat!" she cried, running down the riverbank to his left. "Please, Pat, don't jump!"

Death is even stranger than invisibility, Pat thought lazily, until he realized he hadn't yet let go. He opened his eyes and saw Louisa twenty feet below him, messy ponytail, dirndl skirt, and all.

She was staring up at him. *She can see me.* The thought jolted Pat, nearly made him lose his grip. Louisa's mouth was moving. Was she praying? Pat couldn't remember if she was a religious type. When Louisa had first started, she'd been friendlier, he remembered now, and she would drop by his office and chatter about her life. But he'd ignored her. He had work to do, work that could distract him from the ways his life was beginning to fall apart. She had seen that Pat had no interest in her small talk, and she'd quieted down, to his relief. The HR reports soon followed.

Now Louisa stood below him, pleading with him not to jump. *She can see me, she can see me, she can see me.* The thought echoed in his head like a prayer of his own. *She could always see me.* The thought was so astounding, he wanted to roll in it, soak it up, wear it like a warm blanket.

A crowd had begun to gather, following the arc of Louisa's arm as it pointed out the lonely man above the water. Traffic across the bridge behind him slowed and stopped.

"Okay," he said finally, and climbed back over the railing. When he reached the ground, Louisa led him back to the bench he had vacated—how long ago was it? Fifteen minutes? An hour? Pat Conley didn't care. It was a lifetime ago. This time, she sat next to him. The crowd began to disperse, hurrying back to their cubes, back to normal. But still Louisa's hand rested in his.

22. BAWMING THE THORN
by Vonnie Winslow Crist

Humming a sprightly tune, Nana clung to her wheelchair as Kylie wheeled her nine times around the hawthorn rooted in the far corner of her mother's mother's backyard. Luckily, her grandmother weighed less than a hundred pounds, otherwise Kylie wasn't certain she could've managed to quickly circle the tree nine times on a muggy July evening. But Nana insisted three times three was the magic number when participating in ancient ceremonies.

As Kylie leaned on the wheelchair's handles and caught her breath, her grandmother gazed lovingly up at the hawthorn.

"It's beautiful," whispered Nana. She tilted her head back to admire the flowery garlands, ropes of leaves, and bright ribbons they'd hung on the tree's lower branches. "Your great-great grandmother bawmed the thorn in England with her grandmother when she was a child."

"So you've said."

"In those days, every town had a Guardian tree. Oak, thorn, holly, birch, willow. It didn't matter."

"That was a long time ago, Nana."

Kylie sighed. She'd lived with Nana since she'd graduated from high school, and had assisted her in bawming the thorn three Julys now. Each time, she'd help gather the greenery and blooms that would be woven into long strands for draping on the old hawthorn. Each time, she'd cut silky ribbon into six-foot lengths for tying onto the tree's boughs. And each time, she'd heard the same stories about how her ancestors had bawmed the tree in Appleton Thorn.

"Guardian trees are special," said Nana. "Their roots go deep and reach out to the young trees around them. Guardians share nutrients and knowledge through the tiniest of their rootlets. And when it's time for them to die, they give away all their life essence to the surrounding trees."

"Very generous." She glanced at her watch. A few more minutes of tree talk, and she'd push her grandmother and her wheelchair inside.

"But they don't just protect their fellow trees."

Here comes the weird part, thought Kylie. As a Science-Education student, she believed in the inter-connectivity of many species in the forest. She also knew the planet needed trees to keep the air clean, assist in preventing erosion, and help with the climatic greenhouse effect. That said, she didn't for an instant buy into her grandmother's folklore. And she certainly wouldn't be sharing any of Nana's foolishness with her students when she began student teaching in the fall.

"Those who honor the Guardians will be remembered by the trees." Her grandmother sighed. "I wish I could spend the night leaning against the hawthorn, my head resting on her trunk. Oh, what wonderful dreams I'd have."

"I don't think that's a good idea in this neighborhood," she replied, and swatted at an insect helping itself to a meal at her expense. She'd have an itchy welt on her forearm by morning. "Mosquitoes are out. Means we need to head in..."

"Where you going, ladies?" said a man as he stepped from behind the butterfly bush near the back door of Nana's house.

Kylie turned her grandmother's wheelchair so they squarely faced the speaker. She swallowed hard as she realized he stood between them and the ramp into the house.

"You're trespassing." Nana jabbed the air with a forefinger. "Leave."

"Don't think so," replied the man as he stepped closer, blocking their way not only to the ramp and the safety of the house, but to the cell phone she'd carelessly left on the porch.

Kylie tilted her head. There was something off about the man's appearance.

"Goblin," hissed her grandmother. "I've seen your kind creeping out from the culvert across the street."

"Nana, not now." The last thing Kylie needed to deal with was her grandmother's fixation on goblins sneaking into the city set on robbing and harassing the *regular people*. Still, the guy looked wrong somehow.

"You shoulda minded your own business," warned the man. He cracked his knuckles for emphasis. "We can't have you spreading no tales. Somebody might take you serious. Believe. And that wouldn't do. It'd make it harder on us."

Holy moley! The guy hadn't denied Nana's assertion, rather he'd confirmed it. Kylie considered what to do next as the goblin-man took another step closer. Even if anyone nearby had their air conditioning off and windows open, she knew they'd probably ignore screams, assuming they came from some kids playing in the alley. No phone. A wheelchair-bound grandmother to look after. And nothing but a pair of garden shears in her pocket.

Wait! *Empty hands*, she thought. A true master of karate fights with empty hands. But she knew despite two years of classes, she wasn't a master of karate or of any other martial art. Well, desperate situations called for desperate measures. She pressed her lips together and moved from behind Nana.

"Don't, Kylie," cried her grandmother as Kylie stepped forward, brought her left leg up as if preparing to snap it out in a kick, and then, quick as a snake-strike, she withdrew the garden shears from her pocket.

With a loud, exhaled "Ha," she attempted to shove the steel blades between the ribs of the goblin. For a second or two, the creature's flesh resisted the blades' thrust, but after another "Ha," and the accompanying surge of strength, she felt the blades sink in.

The goblin wailed.

Whether from surprise or fear or both, Kylie stumbled back.

The goblin grunted, lowered his eyelids half way down, and grinned. "It ain't so easy as that."

The mannish creature continued to grin as he pulled the offending shears from his chest and tossed them over the wall that surrounded Nana's yard. The garden tool clattered as it struck the sidewalk, then bounced onto the cement surface of the alleyway.

She took several steps away from the goblin, remaining in the crouched-and-ready stance. Garden shears gone, it looked like her miserable karate skills would have to do. She focused on keeping her center of gravity low, her arms raised and before her, and her fingers extended and pressed together.

My empty hands are weapons, she thought. *Weapons for defense. Weapons to protect Nana and me.*

But even if they somehow managed to get safely inside this time, she knew their safety was temporary. They'd stumbled upon a goblin invasion of the city by happenstance, and that knowledge threatened the goblins' plans.

She studied the face of the creature smirking at her. To the uninitiated, he would have looked like a man—a man with slightly irregular features, but a man nonetheless. They'd have been wrong. If Nana's warnings had been correct, and now Kylie had reason to suspect they were, the streets of their city were crawling with goblins and their allies. Goblins who got their thrills from muggings, murders, and mayhem.

And there it was, just as her grandmother had claimed for years: the rise in crime and the apparent violent turn of human society had less to do with video games, and more to do with the thinning of the barriers that held the dark residents of Faerie on their side of the portals.

As three more goblins slunk from around the corner of Nana's house and joined their wounded comrade, Kylie backed up until she was beside her grandmother. If this was the end for her, she wanted to be close to the most important person in her life. And that's when she noticed the chanting.

Soft as a breeze rustling leaves, Nana was calling to her Guardian tree for aid.

"Ain't going to help, old woman," jeered one of the new goblins. "Trees is deaf. Don't care no more about womenfolk."

A fifth goblin climbed over Nana's stone fence and into the backyard. He was bigger than the first four, and he held a machete in his hand. "Let's get it over with," he snarled. "There's more than these two that needs killing tonight."

And that's when Kylie knelt down, clasped her grandmother's frail hands, and joined Nana in beseeching the hawthorn for assistance.

The goblins laughed and surged forward. Then they stopped, a look of horror frozen on their almost human faces.

From behind and above Kylie and her grandmother, creaks and

groans emanated from the hawthorn. The tree leaned forward, grabbed the five goblins with branchy fingers, wrapped its wooden appendages tightly around the squirming faeries, and squeezed.

Too surprised to move or speak, all she could do was hold onto Nana with her mouth open and eyes wide. A few seconds later, the goblins' limp bodies dangled above them. She felt queasy when the crunch of bones breaking filled the air. But at least the goblins had died quickly, barely having time to utter a scream, and more importantly, the way into the house was clear.

Nana pulled her hands away from Kylie's and pressed them together as if in prayer. Her dark eyes sparkled as she whispered, "They're coming."

"Who?" Kylie couldn't imagine what was making the approaching drag-thump sounds.

"Why, the Guardian's charges," her grandmother replied, as if it was the most obvious thing in the world. She'd barely gotten the word *charges* out when fifteen or sixteen younger trees marched up to the stone wall surrounding Nana's yard.

Kylie recognized the Bradford pear trees. They lined the sidewalk on this side of Monument Street, and offered shade to pedestrians as they went about their workaday world activities—pedestrians who chatted or texted on their cell phones as they hustled down Monument, rarely, if ever, glancing at the Bradford pears. Without a word, the Guardian deposited the goblins in the outstretched limbs of the pear trees, then gestured towards the culvert located on the vacant lot across the road.

Kylie stood up, still dumbstruck, and watched as the Bradford pears nodded, lumbered over to the lot, tossed the bodies on the ground, and proceeded to tear them to shreds. When the deadly fairies were nothing but small pieces littering the dirt, the pear trees sucked the liquid from the fleshy bits. Still in a daze, but drawn to the carnage like a rubbernecker at an automobile accident, Kylie stumbled to the stonewall to get a better view of what would happened next.

After a nod in the direction of the Guardian hawthorn, most of the younger trees shuffled back to their square of earth and re-embedded their roots in the soil. The only evidence of their adventure was the edges of nearby sidewalks, which were slightly lifted.

The remaining pear trees swept the dried goblin flesh, bones, and teeth into the culvert, then pushed several large rocks across the entrance. After nodding at Nana's hawthorn, they, too, shuffled to their square of dirt and resumed their normal place in the landscape of the city.

And that's when she noticed her grandmother. Nana was on her feet, holding onto one of the Guardian's branches, dancing. The wheelchair was on its side. Nearby lay Nana's orthopedic shoes and support stockings. Her grandmother's bun had come undone, allowing her white hair to float around her face like a halo as she twirled to a tune Kylie couldn't hear. There were fireflies pulsing an eerie green lightshow around Nana, and every plant in the yard had turned its blooms to face her grandmother and the hawthorn.

Unwilling to break the spell that enchanted the backyard, Kylie stood still as stone and watched a miracle. After a few minutes, Nana looked at her, smiled, left go of the hawthorn branch, and slumped to the ground.

Kylie rushed forward, knelt, and lifted her grandmother's head into her lap.

"I'm leaving."

She brushed the wild strands of white hair back from Nana's face. "Don't be silly. We'll get you back into your chair and inside—"

"Now, it's up to you to watch for goblins and bawm the thorn."

"Anything you say," she promised as she tried to help her grandmother sit up. "Come on, there's a cup of tea with your name on it waiting—"

"No, dearest," said Nana as she reached out and touched Kylie's cheek. "They've come for me. You must let me go."

Before she could protest, hundreds of twinkling fireflies landed on her grandmother, then lifted up in unison and soared through the festooned limbs of the hawthorn. And for a moment, amidst the flowery garlands, ropes of leaves, and bright ribbons they'd hung earlier on the hawthorn's lower branches, Kylie saw Nana laughing.

As she watched, her mother's mother grew thin as mist and sailed skyward with the fireflies. She glanced down at the tired body she cradled, and knew without checking for a heartbeat or exhaled breath that Nana was gone.

"But you are not alone," the hawthorn seemed to whisper. "I am here."

And before Kylie went inside to call the authorities, report Nana's passing, and begin the funeral plans, she rested her head against the Guardian's trunk, closed her eyes, and dreamed the most wonderful dreams.

23. LOSING ASHLEY
by Angeline Trevena

Lorna sat on her usual bench, smothered by her oversized coat. Despite the cold weather, the park was full, the air filled with laughter and screams. They were screams of happiness and excitement, but Lorna flinched every time.

She could see the parents looking at her, and knew what they were thinking. But she had to be here; she had to know that life continued, that not every hope ended in death. Wiping a tear from her cheek, she stood up. She'd be back soon enough. She couldn't stay away.

As she pushed the front door closed behind her, Clay stepped out of the living room, his arms folded across his chest.

"I don't suppose I even need to ask where you've been, do I?"

Lorna ignored him, shrugging her coat off and hanging it up on the hook. She tried to duck past him, but he moved to block her.

"You have to stop this. It's not healthy. Plus you'll probably end up getting yourself arrested."

Lorna rolled her eyes. She'd heard it a million times before, and not only from him. "Leave me alone. Dr. Haskell said I need to give myself time and space to grieve."

Clay grabbed her wrist. "It's been eight months. It's time you returned to your life, returned to work. A bit of normality will help. You didn't die."

She looked at him; his face was unfamiliar through the blur of tears. "Yes I did." She wrenched her arm free. "And if you don't realise that, then you don't know me at all."

She climbed the stairs and slipped into the nursery. She picked up a blanket and nuzzled her face into it, although the scent of her daughter had long-since faded.

The room was waiting to be filled again. The mobile wanted to turn, the toys wanted to be squeezed, the monitor wanted to listen. They'd been given a brief glimpse of joy, but it had been ripped away all too soon. Lorna looked down at her hands. Why hadn't she held on tighter?

There was a gentle knock on the door, and it edged further open. "Can I come in?" Clay asked.

Lorna shrugged and turned away from him.

"I'm just worried about you," he said.

"Well, I'm worried about you. If you don't understand what I'm going through, if you're not feeling the same, then you couldn't have loved her like I did."

"I can't believe you'd even say that." Lorna heard the crack in his voice, and her stomach filled with the ache of guilt. "Life goes on, and one of us has to take care of the everyday things. Paying bills, food shopping, surviving. I have to do that for the both of us. I don't get the chance to wallow in my grief. Perhaps I would like to go to the park and stare at the other children, to obsess over the fact that I'll never see Ashley grow up like that. Perhaps I'd like to sit in here for hours on end, just staring at her cot. But I have to carry on, Lorna. I have to because you won't."

She looked at him; his jaw clenched, his eyes full of tears. She frowned; maybe he was right.

It had been a hard day. Lorna had finally called a support group Dr. Haskell had recommended. Telling someone what had happened made it real all over again. Sometimes she could pretend it was just a nightmare that she would wake up from someday.

"I hope I can do this," she said to Clay.

"You'll surprise yourself, I bet." He squeezed her leg and smiled broadly. "I'm really glad you're doing this. I'm proud of you."

Lorna smiled and turned back to the television. It may as well have been static. She stared at it, like she was supposed to, but she didn't see or hear it. This was what she did; just acting like a human, pretending to live. She felt like she would be pretending for the rest of her life.

One program blurred into the next, and Clay's head lolled back, his mouth open. As he snored gently, Lorna eased herself up from the sofa, pulled on her coat, and quietly clicked the front door closed behind her.

She stepped into the cold air and the acid-orange glow of street lights. They lit the pavement in spotlights, quietly hissing.

The park was a different place after dark; with the children asleep, it belonged instead to the drunks and the homeless. This was its private life, its life behind closed curtains. Maybe everything was merely pretending to be a better version of what it really was.

She settled into her usual spot, despite the damp seat, and looked at the empty swings. Nothing had ever looked so sad. This place was designed to be full of life, and it disturbed her to see it so completely empty. Her house was this play park. *She* was this play park.

A movement pulled her attention to the slide. In the darkness beneath it, something moved again. And then it whimpered. Lorna crept forward, straining her eyes. It looked like nothing but a pile of rags, but then there was a chubby hand, its fingers reaching, grasping. Wrapped up in a thick, grubby blanket, the baby looked up at her as if it had been expecting her. It reached out and cried again. *Take me home*, it said. *I'm yours now.*

Lorna picked it up, moving slowly, as if any sudden movement could make the child disappear. She smoothed down its wispy hair, walked her fingers up its tummy, tickled its toes. She rediscovered a heaven she had thought was closed to her forever.

As Lorna hurried home, the baby tucked inside her coat, she knew what Clay would say. She stared up at her front door, wondering if she should just carry on walking, start a new life. But her home was ready for a baby; it needed one, just like she did. They had all dared to hope.

She walked up the steps and pushed the door open. Clay stood in the hall, his coat on, his keys in his hand. He drew her to him, burying his wet face into her neck.

"I found a baby," she said.

"Thank god," he replied. "Thank god."

In the following seven years, they moved five times—different streets, different cities—driven by fear and paranoia. They kept to themselves, always packing up whenever people started asking too many questions. Ashley was much darker than his parents, with dark hair, brown eyes, a perpetual tan, and questions about that always

150

came up sooner or later.

This time, they found themselves in a quiet, suburban street. The kind where neighbors borrowed things from one another, and the children played outside. Ashley pressed his face against the window of the moving van, eyeing the street outside.

"You see," Lorna said, "you'll like it here. Look, there's a little boy living right next door. He looks about your age." She turned to Clay. "I have a good feeling about this street. I think we'll be happy here."

"I hope so," he said, smiling back.

Lorna leaned back in her chair, watching Ashley play in the back garden. While he was sociable and quick to make friends, he often chose to play alone, chattering away to himself. Lorna saw nothing odd in it; she had been a loner as a child.

Ashley turned to her and shot her a smile full of teeth. He was perfect in every way. Over the years, Lorna had come to believe less and less that someone would have abandoned such a beautiful child, deciding that Ashley had been left there especially for her to find, that he had been made just for her. The universe had realized it had made a mistake in taking her first baby, and she had proved that by being the most devoted mother ever.

She never voiced these thoughts to Clay. Although he acted the part of the loving father, she knew that he had never quite bonded with Ashley like she had. He hesitated before kissing him, stiffened slightly when they hugged. No one else would even notice, but Lorna did. He had never fully accepted Ashley as his own.

She looked up again, and found the garden empty. Standing, she scoured the shade behind the trees and bushes, and then saw his head moving in the playhouse. She wandered out through the patio doors and down onto the lawn. He didn't look up. He was deep in conversation with someone. Lorna crept closer.

"She's a wonderful mummy, you chose well for me.....I'm very happy.....Yes Mata.....I know where I came from.....I know, Mata, we'll be together soon."

Lorna wrenched the playhouse door open and pushed her head inside, a maniacal smile on her face.

"Who are you talking to, darling?"

Ashley spun around. "No one, Mummy. Just playing."

"Good boy,"

She crossed back to the house, a memory triggering in her head. In the dining room, she pulled out a drawer of Ashley's pictures. She ripped through them, scattering them all around her. She held one up. In front of a drawing of a house stood four people, their names written below them. Ashley. Mummy. Daddy. Mata. Mata's head was cocked at an odd angle, as if her neck were broken. Her face was a blank, grey circle; no eyes, no nose, no mouth.

In another drawing she was embracing Ashley. Another had her floating in the top corner of his bedroom while he slept. Another where her face was peering out from behind Lorna's shoulder. She was ever-present, always with her neck bent, her face blank and gray.

Lorna put the pictures down on the table, gripping the back of a dining chair as a dizzy spell swept over her. She looked out into the garden where Ashley was spinning around, his arms outstretched as if dancing with an invisible partner. She looked back at the pictures, screwing the paper into her fists.

"He's my son," Lorna whispered. "You gave him to me, don't you dare try and take him back."

She took the stairs two at a time, and yanked the airing cupboard door open. Pulling blankets, towels and sheets from the shelves, she discarded them around her feet like a multi-colored ocean. At the very back, she found it. The blanket he had been wrapped in when she'd discovered him. She had to destroy it, burn it.

There was a brazier around the side of the house, out of sight of where Ashley played. But as Lorna pushed the blanket into it, she spotted writing; a name scrawled onto the fabric with a marker pen. She peered at it, stretching the blanket between her hands. KEVEN MORALES.

She could hear Ashley laughing, calling out "Mata! Mata! Mata!"

The Google search on Keven Morales brought up an entire string of newspaper articles. It appeared he got picked up for being drunk and disorderly on a regular basis, but there was burglary too, fraud, possession of drugs. No kind of father, if that's who he was.

Morales, officially of no fixed abode, is well known by locals as being from the traveler camp just outside Leewater.

Lorna knew it well.

The air carried sweet-smelling smoke, mixed with the thick smell of exhaust. There was food being cooked: meat, onions. Music, a guitar accompanying a chorus of singers, played somewhere. As she

152

passed the caravans, people hung out of the doorways and watched her. Children began to gather behind her, to follow her through the camp site like a parade. They were a mass of color and excitement, barely indistinguishable from each other. Lorna couldn't even pick the girls from the boys.

"Hey lady," one of the children said. "Where you going?"

"I'm looking for someone. Do you know Keven Morales?"

"Yes, I know him." The child puffed up with pride. "But he's away at the moment. His Nana's here though, do you want to see her?"

"Yes please. Can you show me where she is?"

"Sure, sure." The child skipped ahead of her, dancing amongst the caravans. They kept turning back, checking that Lorna was still following. Standing a little distance from the rest of the camp was a small, squat caravan. An awning protruded from one side, hung with wind chimes, bunches of herbs, strings of bells, and wooden carvings. Under this sat an elderly lady bundled up in several layers of clothing. Her skin was dark and weathered, her white hair thinned away in patches. But her eyes were young and bright, as if she had borrowed them from someone else.

When she saw Lorna, she gestured her over. "Come, come, I knew you'd find your way here eventually."

"You know who I am?" Lorna asked.

"Of course, of course. Sit yourself down." She gestured to a folded patio chair.

As Lorna assembled the chair and settled into it, the children organized themselves into an orderly line, and the woman pressed something into each one's open hand. They ran away whooping and screeching.

She looked up at Lorna and winked. "Vitamins. So how is the child?"

"How do you know?"

"I watched you take him. He's my great grandson; I wasn't going to leave him there to fend for himself, and Keven would have been quite happy for the poor thing to die of exposure."

"What about the mother?"

The woman shook her head slowly. "There was an accident." She sighed. "The child should never have been born. There's an old family curse that falls on any first-born son. We have been fortunate for generations and produced girls first. But Keven fathered a boy, and you have found us just in time. I knew the gods would lead you here before it was too late. I've been working on that." She raised her eyes upwards, whether to the articles hanging above her, or beyond that to the heavens, Lorna didn't know.

"And don't tell me that you don't believe in curses," continued the woman. "Of course you don't; you've never lived with one. People have forgotten about them over the years. They've fallen out of fashion, but this comes from an ancient feud. It's strong, and before the end, you will believe with all your heart. You love the boy?"

"He's my son."

"Then you will do anything to save him? Because you will have to do something you never imagined you were capable of." She leaned forward and took Lorna's hands in hers, her skin like creased silk. "Your boy will not see his eighth birthday."

"What?" Lorna's voice barely managed a whisper. "What can I do?"

"There is a way to transfer the curse into another."

"Me. Transfer it into me."

The woman shook her head. "Any mother would give her life for her child, but no. It cannot be you. It can only be transferred into another child. An eight year old child. It is the only way to save your boy."

Lorna looked at her shoes.

"They must sleep in the same bed. Top to tail. Split this under their pillows." She handed Lorna a bunch of dried flowers. "That's all there is to it."

Lorna looked at the crumbling plant in her hands. "You say that as if this is easy. Condemning another child to death."

"Will you do anything to save yours?"

Exactly a month before Ashley's birthday, he woke with a temperature. It was mild at first; a slight headache, a little tummy ache, but it became steadily worse. Two weeks later, he could barely keep a meal down. He was rapidly losing weight, his eyes sunken and rimmed with deep shadows.

Terror ate its way through Lorna's body. Every morning she looked at her ageing face in the mirror, telling her reflection "Curses aren't real. It's just a coincidence. He's going to be fine."

"This is not just some bug he's going to shake off anymore," Clay said. "I'm taking him to the hospital."

Lorna grabbed his hand. She knew the doctors wouldn't have a diagnosis, or a cure, and talking to a doctor would make it more real than she could bear.

"One more night. Please. Look at him, he's absolutely exhausted. Let's take him in the morning."

Clay opened his mouth to protest, but merely sighed instead. "Fine. First thing tomorrow."

"Thank you, honey," Lorna whispered.

She wandered out into the back garden where Ashley was sat in a chair, a blanket laid over his knees. His heavy eyes opened and closed with the nodding of his head.

She was losing him, and she couldn't deny it any longer. He was barely more than a ghost already. Her heart ached with love for him; it was almost too heavy for her to carry anymore. Tears scratched at the back of her eyes. She ruffled his hair, running her hand down over his hot cheek.

A breeze moved through the garden, scattering dried leaves. Lorna looked over at the trees as they rustled together. Standing between them, her blank face cocked to one side, was Mata. *I'll look after him now*, the wind said.

Crossing to the fence, Lorna stood on tip-toes and peered into the garden next door. "Mr. Everett," she called out, waving. "We were just wondering if Luka wanted to stay over? Have a sleepover?"

24. DAREFUL THINGS:
A STORY IN FIVE VOICES
by Helen Ogden

<u>Sionne, the mother</u>

Furious. I cut and cut as strands of hair fell from my scalp. The danger gone, the last of my long hair patterned the floor. My body sagged with the ache of memory.

I had savaged my hair into a rough-hewn bob. The tips of my fingers, stained arterial red from the festival paint, shook with rage and inexperience.

"Never again, not now, not ever shall I dance. I shall marry someone so far away from this life that there will be no going back."

My wrists itched with the temptation to conjure up more magic; to dance and preen and shake out whatever slaked my bones. I took to unlacing the binds at my waist first and then, too frightened by the vomit marks all over my dress, I began to rip the black silk from my shoulders until only the roses garlanded into my hair remained. The smell of flicker-fire and curdled sugar rolled over my tongue.

Later, as I expected it to, the rich, complicated center came, and then the smell of my blood betrayal was unbearable.

<u>Carlotta, the daughter</u>

Untold rhythms often bristled my skin as I lay in my ribboned cradle at night. When they stopped, I noticed their loss like a chasm within the chambers of the heart. And I knew then that it was all my mother's doing.

Sionne was always separate; bewitching in parts, gathered up into herself in others. Even in my infancy, she unwittingly bestowed gifts onto me; those unravelling tastes from a dareful world translated into the clap of a hand, a gesture, the twist of a wrist.

"You are a funny thing."

I was called upon often in my infancy, chased away making step after step. I would catch a latent horror in my mother's expression, then see it die away.

Clacking objects fascinated. I took to humming made-up rhythms, which caused frowns and heated syllables between my parents.

"Not in front of the infant!"

Nothing in front of the infant, who was a moth on the shoulder of her mother, casting her mother's moves in another skin, in another supple body.

To me it was like cracking open a whorl of living parts full of mother secrets: the head, the heart, the beating, pulsing guilt. Yes, I knew how to recognize guilt early. I knew its warm, liquid tang very well.

I am seven when I become aware of the sweet smell my limbs create whilst casting the dance, the intense gnawing fascination in my heels, the cruel flick my drawn-out long hair makes whilst circling the wood of the platform outside. Sionne's gaze falls to my long hair often, and I bow to her, as if unconsciously pleading, "leave it alone."

I spy on Sionne. I call her that in my head, nowhere else. She is impenetrable from one angle, a cautionary image that slips from my index finger as I try to trace her image in the light. When she lays her fingers across her forehead one night I rest my hands on her knees to see what she does, but her eyes are closed. Her head, and all that is in it, is closed.

Her nostrils flare. I can't do much tonight, she utters. The smell is upon her. I know it is the smell; by holding her, I am swathed in it also.

Lilliana, the Cousin

"Do you know how to dance?"

I ask my cousin Carlotta this as soon as I arrive at the house of

Sionne and Jack. We dance, flaunting and flourishing ourselves. I teach her to do it.

I am here to stay—sent by Loriel, my father. I am too much for Sionne. I can't be trusted to pass on the skills of the dance. My aunt refuses to give her permission despite owing me, owing our side of the family a debt too great. And like a seething squall of acceptance she asks me to visit. Sionne will not visit my house, the House on the Edge. She won't gather up her resources and cleanse the past, oh no.

It is fear that makes them deny the legacy of a dance passed on to us. Fear. The only one without it is Carlotta.

So we begin to walk in step, my cousin and I. Carlotta gets it, as if she's been waiting for me to come along. We walk in step and then after each other, in time, in harmony, and I circle and circle. Carlotta flicks her hair as if that move, that chance to cast and conjure and dance to control the elements, to feel divinity, has been slotted into some distant place in her heart all along.

Carlotta says she calls her own mother Sionne, her real name, to her back, in her thoughts. She is dareful; there is no way I could call my mother out like that, there is no way that I can now.

"What's the date today?"

I know it. I know it above all things. I just want Aunt Sionne to know I know it.

Sionne slams her wine glass down with a crack. Carlotta looks like she has stolen out of her skin to somewhere else. I notice this is a habit of hers. I notice that every time we fall in step, like professionals, her moves are a little bit sharper than mine. The last words I hear from Sionne drop like pebbles across my footfalls on the stairs. Each stone stays there, taunting me.

"Lilliana, go home. Go home, before everything is ruined."

"How can I go home when there is no mother to return to?" I reply.

Should anyone of us forget, later, the sacrifices we made to get here, what the dance has done to my family, they only need look at Sionne's face. It is only a fractional beauty compared to the mother I lost, even when she was beyond the pale.

Carlotta

The year of my conception, a poster appeared on the walls of the town underneath the House on the Edge. Purposefully yellowed, edged with red filigree, it held the focus of all who passed it.

It was a picture of Sionne and her sister-dancer Abrienda.

Lilliana has shown me this. She has pointed out that I am also in the picture—the warm, liquid tang fills my stomach, but I cannot help it.

We own the night when we are together. Lilliana needs me—she hardly lets me out of her sight. The dance carries a sisterhood who stand by if the need arises, to temper whatever the dancer creates; whether it be a heaven or a hell. Lilliana says there has never been and never will be again a marriage of two sister-dancers such as Sionne and Abrienda. This is a chance for me to right a wrong; to dance for my mother and my lost aunt.

My mother's voice loiters on the stairway, in argument with my father.

"But I married you, Jack to take her away from all that. We live in a place that has no part of anything in it! How is she growing into this, this dancer?"

Sionne can't keep it quiet any more. She wants to know where I am getting the skills, the twists in my wrists, the narcissistic curve in my back, and she only has to look at Lilliana. Lilliana, who enquires every year on the same day, "What day is it today?"

I hear her talk to my father in the darkness. Sionne wishes her niece would leave. She wishes there was a time to explain to me, her Carlotta, about what kind of debt she owes. She wishes that she had married a Prince from the South, someone to hide us both away.

She wishes a lot of things now.

She just doesn't imagine that my cousin will go with me one night into land of bloody soles and dareful things. She doesn't know that I will raise oceans to dance over fragments of her misdeeds and spit upon them, into the dust.

Above all she has no idea that I will be the one leading the escape.

Loriel, the Uncle

If they think it is the dust and the heat-sodden sulfur that keeps me ill tempered, they are wrong.

My knuckles are raw from beating them against the wood of my bedroom door. Our bedroom. Mine and Abrienda's.

The shuttered courtyard's dust sifts through my fingers as I enter into it for the first time in years. I won't go near the spot, won't pacify Sionne by wiping away the trench marks in the ground where she cast her own sister out. Her own, my wife, mother to the wretched Lilliana.

Our home was once filled with courtyard after courtyard of dancers, singers, familiar crowds. We are balanced on the salt-scab encrusted rim of the waterline, and all it would take is One Good Storm.

If they think it is my daughter who keeps me ill mannered, who turns me inside out each night, they aren't looking hard enough. The gossips; the sisterhood. They rally and bang against the shuttered door of the fourth yard.

And when the last candle is almost out, Lilliana returns. She has brought my niece, a brunette, pallid little thing with oyster flesh and a sad tongue. I can't see how the crowds will fall upon her. No sisterhood of the dances will stand for her. I wished her blister-borne when I heard of her birth. But they open the doors, still, and invite the blasted night air in, with its tumult and God knows what else.

"Look upon it, Loriel. I have brought Carlotta back to where she belongs. Now get on it, and send the letters filled with dust, whispers of dareful things. Do it, before Sionne follows and wastes upon us all."

My daughter was never the mild one. She knows Sionne has power. She writes until the bump on her index fingers glistens and raws up. The letters are sent, and as each one is opened, grains of my bloody courtyard stain the invited skins of the onlookers, betrayers, and gossips. Only true family wish they could keep away. And they can't. They just can't.

Carlotta

A white caul is cast upon the ground in all three of my Uncle Loriel's courtyards. After the bleakness at home, I welcome the infusion of sweat and jasmine within his arena. Because this is his arena. Even I know a casting circle when I see it.

The house, if you can call it that, tilts to the sea, as if it is bowing to the elements. The balcony on the outer edge, where the little-

160

infantas practice, lifts you forward, and on rougher days sprays you with sea fret whilst in the coolness of the inner corridors, people move in hushed whispers.

"They are afraid to disturb those in-between," my cousin mutters whilst she teaches me moves she can't even master.

"I suppose you are ready."

Her large eyes, the color of over-ripened wine, look me over with a shrill confidence.

"We are to go together, once you try that on," she continues.

The dress hangs; silk, black. It is dareful in itself.

When everyone has disappeared, I try it on and marvel. And in the air behind me there is a shift of matter, of purpose.

I am waiting, for what Lilliana has told me to do is wait. Until I am alone, and then call out into the coolness of the room.

"Abrienda," I say. "Are you there?"

Shoshanna, Mistress of the Sisterhood

A mire. A complete and utter mire; that's what we have all fallen into. To let two young girls take on something they can't even grasp is too much for me, but I am ordered to be here, as part of my sisterhood duties.

Everyone has arrived on the Edge to see what? A fight? Perhaps. They are all weary for action, this lot. Too long they've sat looking into the ocean that pulls them back and forth. It mesmerizes; some have gone sea-crazy.

This is what they see as Sionne appears, uninvited. She has followed her daughter all the way here. She colors Carlotta's dance with the most beautiful gray, which corrodes and caresses the young girl's blue, curdling, cajoling and finally swallowing it whole as they clap and twist, turn and simplify each other, until only a thin swirl remains. It fizzes and gathers over the gaping fleshy mouths of the sisterhood. It is far beyond us to intervene. We are a horror of women, like a murder of crows. A few hold out their wrists just to be touched by it, by whatever marries life and death together.

Lilliana cries out in her selfishness, but that is all she cries, as Sionne displaces her from the marked circle, and effectively from the marked life of the edge.

Carlotta will not be taken in the same way. Her uncle Loriel sits up from his chair in the upper courtyard, as if things are about to get better, more watchable. His fingers are at his throat. He twitches, becomes pale as his eyes follow his niece. His savior dances through the dust as if it is the only thing that belongs to her.

She dances toward the storm.

There are no traces of the girl Carlotta; we wail upon the gates of Loriel for the lost women of song. Many have seen Loriel's wife Abrienda these past weeks, her colored outline against the dry palm grove; the citric tongues of the sisterhood said she was preparing for a war. The taint among us, for there is always a taint, spoke of ruin. They spoke of the sea so great, despite calm and clear waters.

Lilliana, once full to the brim with solipsism, weeps. She has no furor in her now; it has poured out into the world. She shrieks "Mother, mother, Abrienda, how else can I do this for you? What am I to you?"

What is anyone to anyone when a good storm strikes?

We lay crossed swords onto the courtyards, scattered night-scent, shut off parts of the Edge of the World forever.

The great Sionne cowers

while we gather the dust that holds their song.

25. APRIL'S UNPEACEABLE KINGDOM
by Helen Grochmal

April was sitting at her dining room table working on her shopping list when she glanced out of her patio doors and saw the dog walking down the road in front of her house. April got up and looked hard. She clearly saw it walking; it was a fox, a meandering fox.

She couldn't believe it. She lived in a senior retirement community in the suburbs—why was a fox in the suburbs? She knew the common explanations about animals losing their habitats and so on, but this was different. The fox was not afraid. It didn't look sick. It could have been hunting for scarce prey, but why there?

April kept thinking about the fox; it seemed wondrous to her. April believed it was a girl, and she wondered if she had—what were they called?—vixens. April didn't like that name—she preferred "sweet baby foxes"—and they would be very beautiful ones, if they looked like their mother. Maybe the groundskeepers had chased her family away, or worse. April was lonely living by herself, and she wondered if the fox was lonely too. If the beautiful fox picked her out from all of the other residents to be a friend, she would feel so proud, since one could tell it didn't bestow its attentions on just anyone.

She spent less time watching TV and more on her patio or at her dining room table looking out of her patio doors, which took up one whole wall of her dining area. She asked the universe to let her see the fox again. The fox really hadn't declared her friendship for April, at least not yet, but April was sure she would—she had to. April put her head on her dining room table and cried inconsolably.

April couldn't wait to tell her friends at the community about her encounter with the fox, and dressed with special care for the Ladies' Mixer. She looked in the mirror at her thinning gray hair, unfit body, and broken nails—at least her lips were nicely shaped, though she couldn't see anything else good. She walked her careful old-lady walk to the clubhouse, glad it was near.

These mixers were new to their community, so April didn't know who would be there. A volunteer was making punch by mixing together large cans of juice bought in bulk for such occasions. In her eagerness to tell about her new friend, April was the first resident there. Her face bloomed as she thought of that first magical moment of seeing the fox. The door opened, and a new resident came in. The woman, who looked very robust compared to April, came over in her fitted tan skirt and blouse and newly polished fine leather boots. April introduced herself.

"How do you do?" was the answer. "I'm Mrs. Gertrude Peerbohm. I recently moved in with my husband."

The door opened and April's neighbor Rachel came in, quickly followed by another woman. They sat down, making a circle with the chairs and the couch.

April introduced them by saying, "This is Maribel, who lives way over on the far edge of the complex, and my next door neighbor, Rachel."

Mrs. Peerbohm confidently introduced herself. "I'm Mrs. Peerbohm. I just moved here with Mr. Peerbohm."

"Do you golf, Mrs. Peerbohm? I noticed you walking around the course next to us the other day," said Maribel.

"Oh, yes. I need a partner now that my husband is ill. They should have putting holes here on our lawn; golf would promote good physical and mental health among the residents," said Mrs. Peerbohm severely, looking at April.

It didn't look like anyone else was coming that night, and April was disappointed that the gathering was going so badly. She had imagined looks of envy and pride from half the community at meeting a person who had experienced what she had.

Mrs. Peerbohm broke the silence. "I noticed some gopher holes in that golf course today. Don't they get rid of pests around here? I don't want to live in a slovenly area."

April looked horrified and cried out, "Oh, no! We love animals here!" Then she thought of that little stray cat taken somewhere last spring and was glad that she had said nothing about the fox.

"I should hope they are humane here," said Maribel.

"The birds and squirrels and chipmunks are such fun to watch, don't you think?" April said with desperate enthusiasm. "They are God's creatures, who only want to survive like us," she continued, thinking she didn't want to survive too much longer in this harsh world.

"HARRUMPH!" boomed Mrs. Gertrude Peerbohm.

"SHHHH!" said Rachel to Mrs. Peerbohm.

"It's OK, April," comforted Maribel.

"If you ask me, she needs a stiff drink—unless she is drunk already. I mean, we kill foxes all of the time in England. They say some nonsense about stopping it but, of course, nobody listens. Who could care about a fox?"

"I do," cried April. "There is one here and she is my friend. I love her. She is beautiful!"

The other three women looked appalled. Had April suddenly lost her mind? It was common to forget things here or to repeat them, but nobody suddenly started babbling.

"I did! I did see a fox. She was on my patio or near it. She stopped in front of my apartment, sort of."

"Oh, well, it's gone now," said Rachel. "Don't worry about it."

"It was probably rabid. I will make sure it and anything wild is disposed of properly," said Mrs. Gertrude Peerbolm.

"You can't do that! You just can't!" cried April.

"I guess Happy Hour is over," answered Mrs. Peerbohm sarcastically.

A volunteer, who bore a decided resemblance to an old collie, had obviously been listening to the conversation. While collecting the dirty glasses, she stopped and turned to April.

"My family is from Scotland, Miss MacSelkie. Did you know that a selkie is a shape shifter in legends over there? You could be a mermaid," she laughed.

April looked bewildered and somehow disturbed. "I don't know anything about that" was all she could think of to say.

They left the clubhouse together. Mrs. Peerbohm went one way, the other three the other way, until April and Rachel were alone.

"What did I do?" April burst out. "Did I betray my friend? Will that lady do something to her?"

"No, no. Don't think that. The fox may not come back."

April got to her house, switched on her patio light, and sat, sobbing, at her table. Fantasies of warning her friend and begging for her forgiveness filled her dreams. She awoke in the morning with her head on the hard table and a mark from the table on her face.

April looked out of her door obsessively. Could she communicate with her friend? She remembered hearing of Native Americans talking to animals. She knew why now, but would the fox talk to her?

April was looking out of her glass patio door as usual one day when she glanced up into a tree and saw an enormous bird. She knew it wasn't a vulture. She went to the glass door and was overwhelmed by the huge bird with its talons over the branch, but it disappeared in a flash. It must have been an eagle, she thought, a beautiful creature. She had seen the feathers so clearly but had not seen its face too well.

The experience was overwhelming. April was proud that these special animals came so near her, but were they trying to tell her something?

Yet she was haunted by Mrs. Peerbolm's threats. Nature had blessed her, but she might have answered the blessing by boasting about their visits. "I should have kept their visits to myself. Is that why they are in danger? I didn't keep their faith. I will keep the faith from now on," said April out loud with determination. To prove it, she spent years watching out of her door, keeping the faith.

One day, in her last year of life, April nodded in a lounge chair that she had moved near the large patio door. She knew she couldn't die until she received her forgiveness from the ones who had bestowed the former gifts upon her, though the beautiful animals had never come again.

With days to live, she saw something looking in her patio window. She had been praying the fox would come back, but instead, she saw what she first thought was a raccoon. It was a burnt orange color like the fox, but it had the frame of a little bear. It was nothing she had seen before. She cried out in wonder, "Please let me die now, please. I can die happy now. Thank you, Thank you..." But she did not die.

She saw the little animal for three nights. She told nobody. "I'm keeping the faith," she said only to herself over and over. "Please stay safe, little creature. Go back to your world and take me with you,"

166

she prayed. But she did not die.

They put her on her bed, although she begged to stay in front of her patio window. The creature would never come again, she thought in distress, with medical aides coming in and out. It will leave me here.

As she neared her end, three people making up the residents' visiting committee came to her room to see her. (Mrs. Gertrude Peerbolm had gotten herself appointed President of it by Management. No one could get her removed, although they had tried. The other committee members wished they could kill her.)

They sat on straight backed chairs. April was partially conscious and her mind wandered.

"I saw it! I saw it, strange creature."

"Are you imagining silly animals again?" asked Mrs. Peerbolm.

"Stop!" yelled the others present.

"It must have been beautiful, April," soothed Rachel.

April seemed to be looking at something wondrous above her. "Yes, yes. Thank you, thank you. What are you trying to tell me? What is it I don't know?"

"Snap out of this nonsense," Mrs. Peerbolm was saying as the other old women pushed her out of the bedroom and out of the front door.

They went back to the bedroom to hear poor April saying "Did I tell, did I tell? Oh, no, no, no…"

The others made comforting sounds.

April died saying, "They are real. Save them, save them! Did I tell? Please forgive me…"

April was buried after an hour-long ceremony in the nursing home chapel, although more residents came than usual.

Mrs. Peerbolm couldn't be kept away. "She was delusional, you know," she told anyone who would listen, though she found herself standing alone a lot.

On the day of April's burial, a story appeared on all of the news shows: New species found in Tanzania, looking part cat, part reddish bear, and part raccoon. It turns out that one of these animals had been mistyped in captivity and had disappeared from the Metro Zoo years ago. It was never found, but it had refused to mate with the species it had been put with in the zoo, so the animal would be gone from America. Its bones were never found.

Rachel went to bed that night wondering if April's fox was the enchanted being the runaway animal had chosen to mate with.

Author's Note: One evening, while finishing her exercises, Mrs. Gertrude Peerbolm was passing by the patio where April used to live and was slowly eaten by a giant snail.

26. THE DEVIL'S IN THE DETAILS
By Judi Calhoun

In the primeval forest, on a secluded, un-trampled path, surrounded by trees hiding secrets dark and bantam, whispering in the breeze, I stumbled upon a malevolent stranger wearing a long purple coat and high top hat. From that sharp gleam in his eye and that devilish grin, I knew without proof; he had vetted me with just one single glance.

With that dreadful air of perception, he wore a smug grin, as if to say he owned the answer to every problem that vexed this world, or perhaps just the solutions to my personal tribulation.

The silver metallic orb hovering between us hesitantly drew closer. When my gaze lingered too long on the orb, I caught a sad glimpse of my future: a broken man in trouble.

Some people, most people, smart people, would have turned, ran, and never been foolishly deceived by the likes of this magical devil man, but not me. I was far too often misled by curiosity—a deluded, reckless man chasing rabbits down holes.

"Good morning," he said. The moment he tipped his hat; a few fairies flew out. They lingered near his ears and whispered some secret before they vanished.

"I've been waiting for you, Julian. Today is your lucky day."

I frowned, wondering how he knew my name. He wasn't at all familiar. I wished now that I'd kept an adequate distance, because at that moment, I couldn't move my feet. I glanced down, believing I'd stepped in cement, and yet nothing besieged me, just some unseen powers at play.

"You can become anything you want," he said, spinning that orb that whirled out toward me and lingered. "Simply by making a wish. Rest assured, it would immediately be granted."

"What is the catch?" I asked.

He groaned. "Why do people ask that question?" He stretched out his hand, and the orb returned to him. He balanced the sphere on the tip of his finger; he leaned closer, gazing deeply into it as if reading.

"Your future is bleak, Julian. It doesn't look as if your life will ever amount to anything. What a pity that you failed the bar exam," he said. "Mmm, after spending all that money on law school, what a shame. Then there's Sandra, pretty Sandra with the golden hair; she'll marry your boss. You hate your job working in the complaint department for several department stores." He let out a long sigh. "Aw, too bad, it looks as if you'll never win the lottery; might as well save your money now. However, your friend Dennis will win very big. He'll purchase that red Corvette you've always wanted. Oh, and your cousin Joanne will sign a major book deal with a New York publisher, but your dreams of working in litigation will go up in..." Smoke swirled around the sphere as it vanished. "Well, you get the idea."

"Who are you?" I asked.

"Ah, and there's the next irritating question," he said. The gleaming argent orb materialized just above his open hands. "What difference does my identity make in the scope of things, Julian? I offer you a wonderful life by granting you one wish, one opportunity to change everything. Don't be so small as to seek my identity, because I will grant you that wish, instead of making you a lawyer with his own firm or any job your heart desires. So, tell me your secret fantasy, because, unfortunately, the only way I will ever know it is to hear it from your lips the moment you touch the Oracle orb. All I ask in return is a promise signed in your blood."

"I have to give you my soul?" I asked.

"Let's not trouble ourselves with the sordid details," he said. "Think about it, Julian. When are you ever going to get another offer like this in your mediocre lifetime? Touch the orb, think, and speak your desire."

It didn't take me long to start listing the many needs that tortured my mind on a daily basis. The check engine light was coming on every day now. I had no idea what was wrong with my truck. I was two payments behind on my rent, and just today, I'd received a notice of eviction. I hadn't been laid in three months. My refrigerator was empty. I had no idea where my $245.13 paycheck went every week. My boss was riding me on treating customers with more respect. My attitude was just the sort of thing that could get me fired. This was the best offer I'd had in a very long time. I'd be stupid not to take it.

"I'll do it," I said.

A smile, devious and filled with smug satisfaction, slid across his lips. The Oracle orb moved toward me, until I could see my fish-eyed reflection staring back. I started to reach for it, but paused when magical devil man cleared his throat.

"Before you begin to think and speak your desire, you must first sign." He waved his arm, and from the shadow of his coat sleeve, the pages of a parchment contract flapped onto the ground, rolled out, and then kept rolling down the forest path. "You must sign here." He pointed, and as he did, a silver knife blade grew long from his fingernail.

He grabbed ahold of my right index finger and slid the sharp edge across the skin. I winced when he spread the cut open, and beads of blood formed. He turned my finger over and waited for drops of blood to hit the parchment. The blood spread across the paper, swirling into letters that formed my signature in my handwriting.

"That's all I need," he said. The pages rolled up mystically into his sleeve. "You have until your fifty-ninth birthday before this contract becomes due. However, you can extend your life another ten years if you decide to become an evil dictator. Now, you are ready to make your wish." The orb spun up into the tree branches and came slowly down into my waiting hands.

He held up his finger. "I say this to all my clients: be very careful what you wish for, because you may live to regret it, as so many often do." He chuckled at his own words.

I had one wish. It should have been easy. I remembered when I was younger, innocently believing that one day I'd have this opportunity to make a grand request from a magical genie. Back then, I wanted to become a superhero. I wanted powers, like mind reading and ex-ray vision, but now all that seemed silly.

I wracked my brain, hoping to make the most prudent choice that any candidate had ever made. Then it came to me, bright and brilliant as a star. I closed my eyes and let my thoughts repeat the request. I touched the cold silver ball and said, "wisdom."

Instantly, my brain felt as if it had expanded twice its normal size. I comprehended everything, even the folly of my choice to sign his contract, but it was too late. My benefactor was vanishing, laughing as he disappeared into the ether, leaving behind a thin curling trail of smoky fog.

Months turned into years, and years moved by much too swiftly. All the while, I was enjoying a prosperous life. I took the bar exam again and passed. I won one of the toughest court cases in history, which opened up an opportunity to work at the best law firm in New York City.

With my newfound status and a great paying job, my love life improved. I phoned my friend Dennis and told him I would be happy to front him money, as long as he kept buying lottery tickets; we could share the winnings. Of course, I made him sign a contract, since I already knew he was going to win, and he did. Dennis won three hundred million. I never had to work again, so I moved to the island of Kauai until the anniversary of my final birthday rolled around. I should have been preparing for death by getting my affairs in order. Instead, I was lounging in a beach chair in the sand, a cocktail in my hand, listening to the gentle rhythm of the waves rushing onto the sandy shore.

Something big was swimming toward me, as if a whale was about to beach itself. I nervously sat forward, squinting.

A giant lobster, the size of a human, struggled toward me in the sand. Its shell split open and claws turned into arms as he transformed from crustacean into my magical devil man. He hadn't aged a day, while my middle-aged, flabby belly hung over my belt from the sixty-five pounds I'd gained in my lazy days of wealth.

I didn't move from my ugly lawn chair. I calmly stared off at the sun, which was setting in the orange sky, and took a sip of my cocktail.

"Hello Julian. Your time is up. How do you want them to report your death. Suicide? Accidental drowning? Poison?"

"None of those," I said. "I'm not going to die. I found a loophole in my contract."

Magical devil man cleared his throat. "I have only one loophole: you become an evil dictator. My dictator alarm clock never went off.

Therefore, you do not qualify for a ten-year extension."

"I found another way around it."

"I don't understand," he said, frowning.

"You see, the entire time that I was asking for wisdom, I was also thinking, planning, scheming. I desired wisdom for one purpose only: to subvert your powers by taking your job. You said I could have any job. Well, I wanted your job. And didn't you tell me that thoughts were just as powerful as saying the words?"

"You're much smarter than I thought," he said, removing his hat to wipe perspiration from his forehead with his jacket sleeve. "However, Julian, you neglected to read the fine print. It states that you cannot take my powers from me."

"Yes, very true," I said. I snapped my fingers and watched as the silver orb, almost orange from the afternoon light, swirled into my hands. It was mine now, and floated just above my hands. "Law school taught me a great many things about contracts. I spent the past thirty-seven years studying my convention until I found that loophole."

The magical devil man face turned red with frustration. "Give me back my orb!"

"The orb belongs to the man with the magic."

"You do not have the magic. I do! And by the stars, there are no loopholes in your contract."

"You're wrong. There are loopholes in almost every contract. Nothing is ironclad. You see old man, you had the coolest job of all, and the only job that I wanted. Line six paragraph 899.5.1 states that I cannot take your power, but what it neglects to state is much more important." I sat forward so I could joyously revel in the disappointed look I saw on his face. "There's nothing in my contract that precludes me from asking for your job, and of course, as a by-product of your job, I also get your power. That's why the orb came to me; I'm the new progeny of power."

"Lawyers! You are the scum of the earth," growled the magical devil man as he spit in the sand. "How did you find your contract? I keep them secretly locked away. I never allow any of my victims access. So tell me, Julian, what trickery did you use to gain entrance to my records?"

"It wasn't easy," I said. "I tried supernatural locksmiths, wizards, and I even tried learning binary code. Nothing worked until I remembered that first day, when you tipped your hat and the fairies flew out. They whispered in your ear before they vanished. They were promising to file my contract away, weren't they? I figured it all out."

Magical man was pacing in the sand. "How could you know that?"

"I found them. It took me five years. Did you know they are easy to bribe? They helped me to locate your hidden office. I commend you on being so neat and orderly, which made it easy to locate my contract right away."

"No. I didn't think it was possible. No, this can't be true. I've been out-smarted," said magical devil man. "Julian, dear Julian, perhaps we can make a deal. We can, can't we? I could be your assistant. I could teach you all about this job. Please, Julian, I...I know I've already lost my job to a smarter man, but you have no idea what's going to happen to me. I'll be sent to the lower regions, to endure endless bickering from the very people I tricked into signing those contracts. I beg you to stop this atrocity. I don't want them to dump me into Hell's merciless complaint department."

"Sorry, old man. The orb says that's your new job."

"No!" he screamed, his voice resonating as he vanished along with the setting sun.

27. ELF HILL
by Aline Boucher Kaplan

Harno hefted his axe and moved cautiously up the hill as dusk crept through Eythorne Wood. The forest was silent. Creatures that should have been settling with May's evening twitters and calls were instead hiding from a brilliant light no fire had made. Felling the blasted oak had taken longer than Harno had planned, delaying his journey home, but the bright white light ahead held darkness at bay and stopped his tired feet. Something terrible had come to the valley between him and the village.

Slowly, carefully, he peered around the bole of a big chestnut tree, squinting against the glare and struggling to make sense of what he saw. The little valley with its quiet stream was filled by what could only be the Elf Hill of his granny's tales. Its slopes arched from the grass to form a low dome, smooth and shiny as ice. Fear seized his heart as tightly as his hand gripped the axe. Elf Hill, looking just as Old Maurin's stories had described it, lay between him and the village. Harno did not know why it had appeared in this wood or what the elves wanted there. He knew only that he had to get home to protect Luciann and their new babe.

Tearing his eyes away from the hill, he surveyed the valley. He could circle around its north end, staying beneath the trees until he reached the other side, and then speed toward the village. *Run*, the woodcutter told himself, willing his feet to move, to take that first step, but they remained as rooted as the trees.

A low rumble began, rising through the soles of his buskins before his ears heard the actual sound. It felt as though he was standing on Eyford Bridge when a heavy wagon crossed. A high-pitched whine joined the rumble. The new sound, hard and bright, grew louder until it hurt his ears. He clapped both hands over them, mouth opening so far that his beard curled on his chest, as if to let the sound out. Harno forgot to breathe.

This was dark magic, such as he had never encountered in his steady and predictable life. He was a simple man who followed the rules set by the priest and the elders, heeded Old Maurin when she spoke, and carried a pike in the Baron's yearly muster. Now he tried frantically to remember what he knew of Elf Hill.

"It is the work of the devil," the priest had warned from the pulpit. "He will lure you into its shining hell and flay your soul for his dark pleasure."

Maurin the Hag, who always spat after the priest when he passed, also warned of Elf Hill, but for different reasons. "Time runs odd in there," she had said, the fire weaving shadows on her lined face. "If you follow the elves' call—and they will sing you pretty, my lad—you are lost. They'll make your soul dance to their wild tune and long years will pass in an instant before the Little People release you again."

"It's just a story," he whispered. "It can't be real." But now the hill reared up as solid as the village church and amazingly bright, as if the full moon had fallen and sunk halfway into the ground. *This cannot be happening*, he thought. The smells of damp soil and new leaves reassured him that he still stood in the real world. Harno recited the facts as if they would protect him. *I say my prayers each night and go to Mass every Sunday. The one time I saw Baron Tarquin, I knelt promptly and tugged my forelock as is proper.* The woodcutter shut his eyes hard and took five breaths before opening them again.

Elf Hill gleamed brighter than before. It began to open.

First a dark line appeared on the shining slope. It widened like a sly smile into a wedge, which gaped dark as a toothless mouth. For a long moment it remained that way, and Harno's heart pounded. *Will I see the elves? Will they look like devils?*

A figure appeared in the dark doorway and, one by one, the elves came out.

The Little People were no taller than a boy, and delicate. Rich clothing covered their slender limbs, which were adorned with jewels. Their faces were fair and beautiful beyond description. Pale hair floated from under golden crowns in a fairy breeze only they could feel. The elves wandered about, peering into the night-dark woods as if searching for something. With a shudder, Harno pulled back into the chestnut's shadow.

An elf turned, as if it had caught his movement. The others followed its gaze as it pointed a long regal finger in Harno's direction. The woodcutter broke into a sweat despite the cool evening. *Did they see me? If they did, what could they want with a simple woodcutter?* Harno stood as rigid as the tree trunk, afraid to look again.

Long shadows moved in the bright light that bracketed the chestnut's trunk. Harno groaned and said a quick *Pater Noster*. For added protection, he prayed to the Horned God and the Green Man of Eythorne Wood as well. Yet all the deities failed him. Harno felt a pull inside his head, a light touch as irresistible as the river's current. It summoned him. The woodcutter's obedient feet took one step and then another. Compelled, he walked stiffly out of the wood to face a row of elves.

Lights flared on the hill, with white ones marching around the structure's rim while blue ones pulsed at the peak. The elves, wild and beautiful, beckoned him closer. As Harno's feet marched forward, he cursed the stubborn oak that had resisted his axe until almost the last stroke. If not for that, he would be home now, eating supper and watching Luciann nurse Stefan. He would be there to protect them from this awful threat. Instead, the elves had found and ensorcelled him. He tried to hold Luciann's image in his mind, but saw only his own face reflected in the elves' large up-tilted eyes. Harno was stiff with terror, despite the soothing words they spoke so clearly in his head. Like Luciann's cradle song, they urged him to be calm, to be happy, to keep walking.

"No," he protested, but his mouth was dry, and the words emerged as a whisper.

"Be tranquil," soothed the silent voice. "You have nothing to fear."

"Please let me go," Harno begged. "I just want to go home."

"All will be well," the voice replied.

Harno wanted to believe it, but how could he trust any creature that possessed his body and held it in thrall? His feet kept marching, as though they belonged not to Harno, but to the Little People. He was bigger than them, and far stronger. Two swings of his axe would destroy the eldritch creatures, strewing their delicate forms across the grass like bloody flowers. He willed his hand to lift the tool, but it refused to obey. The vibrations in his feet grew stronger, reaching into his bones and spreading up until his ears hurt and his head pounded with pain. Harno's shout of anguish was swallowed by a high whine from the direction of Elf Hill.

The axe slipped from numb fingers and dropped, forgotten, on the bank of the stream. Harno waded across and walked up a smooth ramp to the wedge-shaped door. Slender fingers wrapped around his arm, and black elven eyes swathed him in magic. The woodcutter took a last step, entered Elf Hill, and was lost.

The ramp came up and the door slid shut, closing him away from Eythorne Wood, from Eyford Village, from Luciann and baby Stefan, from everything known and safe and loved. Lights flared around him, illuminating the Elf King's hall. They were brighter than any light he had ever seen but for the sun, and they shone with colors more intense than leaves in the autumn woods. The lights blinked and pulsed; some moved sideways like a snake. They blinded and confused him. He began to pant in fear.

A tone sounded, higher than the church bell and more pure. It filled the round room and echoed in his head. Harno looked up, as if to find a bell tower, but saw only a domed ceiling covered with shapes and textures that he didn't understand.

A voice spoke at his side, and Harno looked down. The Elf King stood nearby, but he had changed. The fine clothing, rich jewels and fair hair had vanished, as if blown away by an eldritch wind. Harno now saw the elves as they truly were, without the glamour of richness and elegance that they had spun around themselves.

They stood no higher than a child of ten years, but were far more slender. Naked, they were covered only by smooth gray skin over a body that had no shape where bones and muscles should be. Harno began to pant in fear.

Their bodies were bad enough, but their heads—oh, their heads! Oval shaped, the heads were too large for the small bodies, yet they stood upright on small, slender necks. Harno searched for features on those smooth faces but found only a small line where a mouth should be, two small holes instead of a proper nose. Yet the eyes were huge, oval and pointed at the ends, slanting upward in a face that seemed too small to hold them.

Those eyes were all one color, and that color was black: black as a forest pool, black as the graveyard at midnight. The Elf King's head tipped to one side and those awful eyes stared at him impassively like a hawk considering its prey.

178

Even a hawk's eyes are golden, he thought frantically. *Even a hawk looks more kind.*

"Welcome to our ship," the Elf King said inside Harno's head. "We have a long journey ahead of us."

At the thought of staying in that domed hill—how could it be a ship?—Harno wanted to vomit. There was nothing beautiful or enchanted here. An evil magic had turned the elves into alien creatures beyond his understanding.

The Elf King's words faded and were replaced in his head by a picture of the stars. Harno gaped at them, uncomprehending, until the stars of the Hunter brightened and the Dog Star at his feet grew even larger. This, the Elf King said, was their destination.

"We have plans for you, Harno," the Elf King added as the Dog Star pulsed brighter still. "Such interesting plans. And so much time to spend together."

Harno screamed.

28. LIKE CLOCKWORK
by Llanwyre Laish

When the Earl announced his engagement to the young and docile Lady Isabella at the Summer Solstice ball, the jeweler's heart shattered. A practical woman, the jeweler had never thought that an Earl would marry her; she had constructed a life out of perfecting bright and beautiful things for other women that she herself could never have, and she had counted the Earl among them. Still, she had long fantasized that the Earl would remain unmarried out of respect for their passionate friendship, which consisted of long wanderings through the palace woods and fiery arguments about the relationship between philosophy and craftsmanship. Their custom was to meet each day at the apple tree at the edge of the palace woods. When they did so the day after the announcement, the Earl was kinder than usual and genuinely dismayed by her tears. Yet when she begged him to help her manage her misery, he put his hands up in the air and excused himself with kind indifference.

Like all good artists, she carried her pain back to her workshop and created. Although her silver-wrapped moonstone necklaces and milky pearl earrings had brought her fame, she had grown bored with the inherent inertness of those creations and had begun to build fantastic sparkling automatons that delighted the court with their lifelike japes. Thus far, she had only created animals, among them a monkey with a ruby-encrusted hat that ate a gilded banana and an eagle that threw open its majestic silver wings to threaten passersby with a sharp bronze beak. Now she crafted her first human, a replica of the Earl that emphasized the weaknesses he worked so hard to conceal: his limp, his wolfish brow, the strange slope of his upper lip, his stiff left wrist wounded by a musket in the war. She worked the metal diligently, focusing on the bright, hot spark of her anger, and the twisted reflection of the Earl soon took shape. Each of his precious imperfections she heightened with a gem: an amethyst on the creature's shoe caught the light when it limped, and a band of emeralds on its hat made its forehead seem to slope more precipitously. Unkindly drawn caricatures of court members were *en vogue* just then—even giggling Lady Isabella had shown some talent for the work—and the jeweler felt sure that her living caricature would make the court laugh and the Earl, a self-conscious and slightly vain man, wince. Yet even in her hatred, she betrayed her love for the Earl, for she gave his clockwork reflection stunning sapphire eyes that seemed to regard the world with kind curiosity.

She sent the clockwork to the Earl's engagement party along with her regrets. The Earl's cheeks burned with shame and rage, but the automaton captivated Isabella. The entire court declared that the jeweler had outdone herself; this mechanical creature truly seemed to have the spark of life, and the court rushed to place orders at the jeweler's shop. The jeweler waited for the temperamental Earl to storm into her store and shout at her about the malicious prank, giving her a chance to speak her mind, but he kept his council, and she cried herself to sleep as she heard her new customers gossip about the extravagant wedding ring he had purchased from someone else.

No lavish planning could hide the Lady Isabella's growing madness, for she had fallen in love with the strange clockwork creature with its sapphire eyes. It was gentler and quieter than her temperamental husband, and its exaggerated imperfections made her feel safer with it than with its overbearing, powerful namesake. Yet the creature spent most of its time at the window, looking out over the town toward the jeweler's shop, for it missed the quick, intelligent hands of the woman who had created it with love and hate intermingled. Isabella's weepy, gracious love felt nowhere near as sharp or real as the jeweler's angry passion. The creature slipped away from the Earl's manor at night to stand at the door of the jewelry shop. The jeweler would find it each morning when she swept the front steps, its face pressed into the front door. Day after day, she raised her hands in kind indifference and sent it back to the palace.

An artist herself, Isabella poured her despair into drawings, capturing the movement of the clockwork man from a hundred angles in swift charcoal cartoons. She made hundreds each day, costing the Earl a small fortune in paper and crayon. A thin layer of sheets constantly carpeted her room, through which the automaton would wade clumsily on its way to the window that overlooked its maker's shop. Isabella's hands grew callused and cracked; she ceased to sleep, dark circles marred her eyes, and her once ivory complexion yellowed. The Earl, who had chosen her primarily for her beauty, loved her less, especially once the court dismissed her because of her weak mind.

This untenable tableaux hung stilly for the remainder of the summer, until, one day, the automaton heard the Earl bitterly complain of the jeweler, "a clever but unmarriageable girl whom I used to meet each day by the apple tree—such folly!" The creature felt the white-hot rage that had fueled its creation and wrapped its thin, metal fingers around the Earl's neck, squeezing until the Earl's fragile life burst from beneath his skin and left his body a limp frame. Isabella discovered them, the clockwork's hands still stretched into the air and its glinting metal fingers marred with blood, and in her love for her husband's mechanical reflection, she hid its crime as best she could. She and the automaton buried the Earl in the palace woods under an apple tree. Sure that her act of devotion would impress the clockwork creature, she cried out in astonished despair when it returned to the window that evening and stood staring at the shop, the starlight bouncing off the curves of its metal face.

When the Earl was missed, the palace guard came to the jeweler's shop to question her. Turned a fatalist by misfortune, she understood that they would eventually arrest her whether the crime was hers or not, so she took the one present the Earl had ever given her—a small, wooden apple-shaped pendant he had clumsily carved himself—and went, weeping, to bury it under the tree as a memorial. When she arrived, she was surprised to find the automaton standing motionless with its face pressed against the tree trunk. Seeing the traces of red under its lovingly-worked silver fingernails, she understood at once what had happened, and this time, when it raised its sapphire eyes to her, she learned the lesson she had meant to teach the Earl and did not turn away in indifference. She kissed it on the cheek and spent the night dismantling the creature and dropping its precious pieces into the river one by one, remembering a beloved discussion she had with the Earl each time she threw a piece of metal into the swiftly flowing water.

At daybreak, the guards arrested her, for the court believed that she had trained the creature to kill the man who had spurned her. She understood the tale's compelling narrative tidiness, so she did not begrudge them their misunderstanding, even when they dressed her in sackcloth and roughly shoved her up onto the guillotine platform. When they cut off her head, the court gave a collective sigh of relief that the "nasty business" was over, and they hid Isabella away in a little cottage at the edge of town. Often, they dredged up the story late at night for visitors whom they wanted to frighten, reminding them that the clockwork man had never been found.

And Isabella, who had done no wrong, remained the only one without respite. She stood for hours each night at the window that overlooked the stream, and during the day, if her nurses did not attend her carefully, they would find her with her face pressed up against the trunk of an apple tree at the edge of the palace woods.

29. AGNETE AND THE MERMAN
by Christina Elaine Collins

The first time she thought about it, the water was green-brown. She paced the rocks. The sea was the best way to go, she was convinced, but not when it was a color like that. She wanted to go in a swirl of blue-green, a hue that would send her off with coolness and serenity.

The second time, the water was blue-black. She paced the rocks. She could wait another day.

The third day, it was blue-green. The true color of the sea. She stared into it, thinking she really shouldn't. She really should stay.

Then his face was there. His eyes were made of that same color—the bluest-greenest of blue-green. He stared at her a while, and she stared back. Then he was gone.

The next day, she watched the water again, still blue-green. His face came eventually, this time emerging through the surface. "Who are you?" he said.

"Agnete. And who are you?"

"Your true love."

"Oh."

He reached for her hand. Their fingers touched. He slipped back under the water. She thought it must be nice to fall away in the blue-green like that.

The next day he kissed her. She didn't tell him it was her first kiss, and he didn't ask. She ran her fingers along his shimmering torso, down to where it faded into scales. Then he asked her if she'd be his.

"You mean marry you?"

He smiled.

She looked back into the blue-green. She could see the reflection of her parents' house behind her. An unspectacular, unremarkable house. Anyone living in it was doomed to be unremarkable too.

"Okay." She nodded.

He smiled again and took both her hands. "Hold still. I need to make some adjustments first."

"Adjustments?"

"Of course. You can't breathe the same way underneath."

He closed her nostrils and bound her mouth so no water could get through. Then he bore her down. She breathed through an opening in her neck. It felt strange, but only at first. She adapted quickly. The world was bluer than the sky, greener than grass.

Eight years and seven children out of her, and not one word out of her bound mouth.

She'd become an excellent swimmer, though.

For eight years she'd swam and swam, gaining more momentum, putting more distance between where she was and where she used to be. Nothing could turn her around. Nothing could throw her off that current, rouse her from that course—except maybe a loud bell.

She heard the bells and shook awake. She knew those bells. Church bells. But there were no churches or bells there underneath with her true love. No, and yet she knew those bells, those sound waves pushing through ocean waves to reach her.

She fretted all morning. She could barely tend to the baby.

What's hurting? the merman signed.

She pointed up. She didn't like his undersea language, even now; the hand signs never translated to what she wanted to say. But she moved her hands and fingers around as best she could, explaining that she wished to visit the land. Would he mind?

Of course he wouldn't mind, he said. As long as she promised to return to the little ones.

The little ones.

Yes, of course, she promised.

He took her up to the surface and unbound her mouth and opened her nostrils. She breathed the newfound openness. No, not newfound—re-found. She agreed to meet him in the same place at dusk. Then his fishtail converged with the green-brown and was gone.

She saw the reflection in the water and turned, squinting up at the cliff. A house. Her old house. With windows. Her window. Rooms. Her room. Had it really been hers? A room of her own. It was hard to imagine now. It was hard to remember what it had been like.

She walked up to the front door. Walking returned to her easily. The moment she knocked, she realized she'd missed the sound. They didn't have the sound where the merman lived. They didn't have doors. There was something about knocking, something about a *thunk-thunk* and a click and someone opening a door to you. There was something about a smile greeting you at a door.

But no one opened this door. No smile greeted her. She waited.

It occurred to her that her parents might no longer live there. They might have moved. Or died. Or forgotten her entirely. Eight years can do a lot.

She turned and wandered back down the cliffside. She walked along the shore to the church where the bells rang. The church where her parents went every Sunday—or used to go. The church where she'd refused to join them one Easter, just days before meeting her true love. She'd stopped believing in God long before that—or maybe she never had believed, only thought she did. Her mother had expressed disapproval in quiet rage, the kind of rage that threatened permanence. Agnete had been seventeen.

She stopped walking. A wave of panic spilled down her back. Seventeen. She had been seventeen.

That meant she was twenty-five now.

The best of her years gone, dissolved in the water like foam. Swallowed and digested by the sea.

She entered the church. A few people knelt in the pews—old men and women with folded hands and crinkly closed eyelids. She sat in the back and listened to the bells. When she was seventeen, the bells had made a sound like promise. She had hardly listened then. Now the sound was different, closer to the ticking of a clock than the tinkling of eternity. The ticking boomed through the church, which looked the same as it had eight years ago. And probably the same as it had at her parents' wedding, her father just shy of thirty, her mother twenty-eight—three years older than Agnete was now.

The bells clanged.

She tried to remember. Her parents had loved her. Yes. And she had been well-off. Well-educated. Well-fed. Well in almost every way.

But she had wanted to leave. Yes, sitting on the rocks day after day, waiting for something to happen, something to break the tedium, she had wanted to leave.

The merman had saved her from the ultimate leaving. But had he deprived her somehow? Had his saving weakened her, flattened her, because it had kept her from saving herself?

Maybe twenty-five was still young.

Maybe she could still do what she had always planned. Finish school. Travel. Fall in love—human love. Maybe it wasn't too late. Maybe it was never too late to reclaim Agnete.

She bowed her head. The bells clanged on. No one here knew about her life in the other world. No one here knew she had a husband or children. It would be easy for her to turn from the sea and never look back, without any consequences. Doing that wouldn't be as easy for other women, whose new lives and old lives would exist in the same world. She was in a unique situation, she knew. If she took advantage of it, what kind of person would that make her?

She knelt in the pew, listening to the bells and waiting for judgment from above. Nothing happened.

At dusk she returned to the seashore, where the merman was waiting. He held out his hand. She looked at it. She looked at the water. It was blue-green, the perfect color, like it had been that first day eight years ago.

But the sea is always blue-greener on the other side.

And you can't know this until you've been to the bottom of it.

She stepped back.

"Agnete?" The merman's eyes widened; his fin twitched above the water, a silent splash. "The children are asking for you," he said.

She took another step back.

"Think of the little ones," he pleaded, reaching out. "Think of the baby in the cradle."

As she turned and walked away, she waited again for some holy voice to condemn her amid the peals of church bells. She waited to feel some moral sting—some pang of damnation.

But she felt only her feet on firm ground and her mouth unbound.

30. IN HER STORIES THERE WERE NEVER ANY CATS
by Jacquelyn Bengfort

At first, I listened hopefully—not that fish have ears *per se*, only rather an arrangement of bones in the smooth envelopes of our bodies. But I lay in a scrim of water, waiting for the vibrations that signify the slamming of a minivan door, the vibrations that meant a key in the lock. I could yet have lived, at that moment. I could have been saved. So I listened, after ceasing a dumb show of struggle, wildly driving myself for a blind hot minute through this thin medium, this air, only to fall again and again upon the window ledge.

No one is coming. But even as I convulse, making splashing slapping sounds too weak for ears of any sort to hear, I cannot complain about this life. My regret—if I can be allowed such a grand thing as a regret—is leaving the girl.

Many claims have been made regarding the physiology of fish, but the most untrue is that we lack memory—that we lack the capacity to remember. I remember it all. I don't think I'm miraculous in this—no, the miracle of my life is not my memories, but rather the girl inside them.

The girl did not care that the general knowledge holds goldfish to be boring pets; that every child, given the choice, will choose a puppy. She insisted, pointing, on tiptoes—"That one, mommy"— and I was swept up, placed in a plastic sandwich bag, gently brought back to this sunlit room. In the car, she held the bag before her face and she and I regarded each other, entranced. It was love.

And that very night, her mother banished her to her room for refusing her fish sticks. She lay hungry on her bed, placed her palm against the glass, and began to tell me her secrets.

I worry about whom she'll tell them to now, even as I feel my flesh stiffening, the convulsing fading to a mute opening and closing of my lips, open-close, open-close, a mummery of protest against this air that is water to the girl. She told me how when her grandma died, they closed her eyelids. That was how she knew her grandma was over, she told me. They shut her like a book. I have no eyelids, nothing to close—I end in a flush. Though, maybe, I'll get the dignity of an empty matchbox, a ring of stones in the grass, a few kind words said. Is it wrong to hope I'll be remembered?

Once, just once, she took me for a walk. She carried my bowl down the stairs and placed it in a red wagon and we made our way around the block. A cat walked down the yard from a neighbor's house eyed me and (I admit) I felt fear.

Here is something true, if you can't believe the rest: everything wants to live. A girl, her fish. A hungry cat. It's how we manage the desire that differs, and a fish—a fish can be life to a cat, for a day.

It began to rain, and we walked on, and the rain drove the cat away. But then, what came after—

The girl fell ill, after that day. We took no more walks. Her hand on the glass warmed my water, and she slept and sweated and tossed, but when she wasn't asleep there were secrets yet, and stories, and in her stories there were never any cats.

She got better, in time. She *thrived*, that's the word they used, and the whispered adult conferences full of words like *febrile* and *pneumonia, pleurisy* and *lethargy*, stopped. For this miracle I am grateful. So, I count two miracles in my time here—the girl, and her life.

She will cry when she finds me, I'm sure of that, and that's more than I need. Her tears are the only water I can hope for, now—a third miracle. I know in my way I was loved more than any of my kind could have hoped. She will know, I think, that it was no one's fault. The ball came through a window open to the breeze, slave to the physics that have shattered so much plate glass so many summers. It lies on the floor, mute and stitched in red, among shards of bowl on the damp carpet. The bard's old slings and arrows come for us all, be sure of that. Even, it seems, for us fish.

The pittance of water left in my world quavers, tries to tell me to hold out, that help is coming, but I am not long for this place. Even if I found myself transported to the sea, a day later I would float solemnly to the surface, wrong side to the sun. Too late. All the water in this wet world cannot save me now. The jelly of my flesh has hardened to resin; my mouth has ceased its involuntary protestations.

I could have been born many things. But I am happy to have been her fish.

31. THE HAVEN:
A SEMI-RURAL FABLE
by Paul Houghton

Mr. Hicks had cinnamon skin and an aura of onions. In his black beret, starched white shirt, trousers tied up with string, and hobnail boots, he resembled an authentic French peasant. With the dark soil under his nails and a light in his eyes, he perched upon his old sit-up-and-beg and creaked towards the village. Garlands of bronzed onions dangled from the handlebars where his front basket was loaded with the earth's mysterious bounties: dark beetroots, emerald cabbages, velvety runner beans. One morning, a villager on the road said, *'Bonjour Monsieur!'* though the nearest he'd been to France was Dover during the war.

Pale, translucent and often powdered with flour, his wife spent her days kneading bread, preparing jams, and perfecting her celebrated pies. Unconsciously mimicking the bees around her latticed windows, she hummed quietly, and when pies or cakes turned out especially well, she might have quaveringly burst into song: *I'm all yours in buttons and bows* or *Oh, sweet mystery of life at last I've found you!*

They had met in a buttercup field when they were twelve, and knew then what they knew now: they would spend the rest of their time on earth together.

"I'll grow cabbages as big as yer 'ead," he'd said, and the yet-to-be Mrs. Hicks was weak with laughter.

When children hadn't come, they put everything into their garden, so green and violet that passers-by stopped to stare. Its lush fecundity pulsed at the eye, and nothing gave the Hicks more pleasure than seeing their rows of spooling greenery bathed in sunshine, that rich fug of the earth rising up; its peaty beneficence.

Solitary and industrious, over decades of long hard years and shorter, easier ones, the Hicks had become so habitual, they were aware of each other as benign presences. Like afternoon shadows, their silences had grown longer, and when they did speak, it was a private language of fragments and single words: "Colander." "Leeks." "Top road." Most of all, they treasured the peace around their words and what they heard there: cool breezes imitating the sea in the top of their trees, the warm, homely chatter of bantams out back, the creaking of their house as it cooled down after a warm day, and the sound of that unsettled world out there, settling.

The Hicks's cottage resembled a dazzlingly white loaf of bread with a burnt crust; house martins flittered from its thatched gables, where a slice of carved oak announced its name: *The Haven.* Inside, all was simple, scrubbed, polished, and orderly; the downstairs rooms with low beams and flagstone floors, the homemade rugs woven by Mrs. Hicks. A dented silver teapot kept warm on the stove while a solemn old clock, like a coffin with a pendulum, tocked without ticking in the parlor. Under the window, overlooking the garden, the round surface of the large oak table was worn smooth as a pebble from decades of hospitality. Its waxed beams bore the dips of visitors' boots. Here Mrs. Hicks served her spectacular teas, and after a stately turn around the outback's botanical splendor, invited guests and casual visitors sampled its produce. There were salads in summer and stews in winter, accompanied by homemade bread and pickles followed by vertiginous cakes and rich dark jams for every palate. Just as the vegetables were out of the soil and on the table that day, the eggs had been laid that morning. Conversations were rooted in the local, and the teapot was never empty.

From the occasional outbursts of their old *Dansette* radio, they knew the outside world was still going the wrong way.

"Riots," said Mr. Hicks, shaking his head.

"Aeroplane crash," said Mrs. Hicks, the pearl of a tear in her eye.

The gnarled, muscular trunk of a great horse chestnut guarded their garden like its keeper; its filigree pyramids of blossom were miniature trees hung upon a tree. Under it, Mr. Hicks toiled beneath an azure sky, just the *chuck-chuck* sound of his spade in the dark soil. Despair had long dissolved into harmony, and it was in this world, so lost to the wider one, that the Hicks immersed themselves—a world that immediately presented itself when they woke up, and subsided when they slept. In a small, safe way they felt they were serving the Earth and God, and beyond the cares of the village, the only wider world they were interested in was Heaven.

The Hicks never had a television, and the only time they'd sat down to watch one was at a neighbor's, during the coronation of Queen Elizabeth II in 1953. It was a miracle then, that silvery-blue vision of the outside world, flickering into someone's living room. In the grim winter of 1973, they had even toyed with the idea of "getting a box" (as Mr. Hicks said) but by that time, they realized television had become malignant, converting the flock from common decency to common indecency. They were shocked to hear from neighbors that television celebrated sex and murder day and night, in documentaries as well as dramas.

"They call it TV now," said Mr. Hicks. "Hmm, might as well call it SV."

Confused, Mrs. Hicks looked up from her needlework. "What's that stand for dear?"

"Sex and Violence," said Mr. Hicks before mumbling, "same thing at my age."

They listened to the radio less; Mr. Hicks might listen to *Gardener's Question Time*, but Mrs. Hicks had given up on *The Archers* in 1977 when, she said, they had started carrying on so.

The Hicks lived five miles from town and never went there; they knew they would neither recognize it now, nor know what to do there. Thirty years ago it had been razed to the ground to make way for an indoor shopping precinct, where they'd heard that real palm trees wilted in the heated square. Now only the church would be recognizable, its drowning spire poking over the roof of a multi-story car park.

But once, because once was enough, Mr. Hicks walked to the

new out-of-town supermarket everyone was talking about. First thing on a fine Spring morning, he set off on the wiry old track that ran through the woods on the other side of their garden. There was a slight frost and all was so supernaturally sharp and splendid, the earth was awesome to behold. The track wound through a thicket of dark pine and a sea of bluebells, misty-blue among the trees.

In half an hour, he came upon the opening to a meadow that riffled like the fur of a cat, stroked head to tail. Upon looking closer, under the burnished rays of early morning sun, he saw that this dewy field was *trickling away*. He crouched, and touching its watery reflection, realized that the trickle across its surface was a fine, lightly bouncing gossamer that covered the entire surface of the field. Like the sea rippling under the sun, this effect, made visible for as far as the eye could see, was the work of spiders across the meadow.

"I'll be jiggered." Mr. Hicks, always excited to see something new that Mother Nature knew all about, took off his beret and shook his head. Conscious of breaking these webs, he walked along the furthest edge of the emerald field, to its far side, overlooking factories in one direction, fields in another. These were divided by a sprawl of identical houses with a gray motorway tearing through the middle. In the foreground was the out-of-town supermarket and approaching, he couldn't believe its size: that of a large town, its vast car park glittering with cars.

Having descended the steep bank from the woods and fields, suddenly he found himself walking between people who were in vehicles or on foot. They stared at him as if *he* was the one from another planet. At its entrance, automatic doors swished open, and from inside, came sharp beeping sounds and the metallic clatter of prison doors as trolleys were herded about. As if it was the war years again, people were lining up in long, miserable queues, but they were loading up far too much. They were spending money as if there was no tomorrow, and looking at this place, Mr. Hicks could believe it.

"Was it very bad?" asked Mrs. Hicks, as if she couldn't tell from his face.

"Ah," he said, "it's another world, and not worth knowing about." He went straight back out again, into the green bathed in gold.

***

Aside from voyages to the village, tending her hens and flowers and, on finer days, taking tea in the garden, Mrs. Hicks was mostly indoors, so redolent of burning oak and baking. On sunny days she kept the back door open so her curious hens could visit. She had given their Sebright bantams the names of children they might have had if God had seen fit: Margaret, June, Eunice and Hylda. Hylda was the jaunty one: defiant and even fiercely friendly. While all had a golden brown coloring with a sheen of emerald on black and laced-edge plumage (as well as impressive raspberry-colored wattles), Mrs. Hicks could tell them apart at a cursory glance. They strutted about, guarding the place while putting on something of a fashion show. Flinty and flirty, Hylda was like a debutant in her finest party dress, and Mrs. Hicks really loved her; she was the only hen that could really be petted, when she was in the mood. But in the world out there, Mrs. Hicks knew she would only be wanted for her eggs, where she would be kept awake all night, in a cage under bright lights, to produce more.

Like her husband, Mrs. Hicks never took for granted that they lived in a world alive with simple beauty and minor miracles. As she plaited her bread loaf and prepared her delicious scones, from here she could see all that she wanted to: wrens, warblers, sparrows and swallows and, tilling the soil in the middle of it all, the figure of her husband, who never came into the house empty-handed. He always bore a punnet of plump gooseberries, cheeky plums, or extraordinary strawberries. He even grew potatoes that sounded like exotic isles or noble people: Sarpo Mira, Belle de Fortenay, King Edward and Duke of York.

On the few occasions when he wasn't working on his garden, Mr Hicks stood by his gate and talked to passersby: small talk and pleasantries, and most importantly of course, the weather.

"Time to cover up your beans I reckon. That Old Jack Frost'll be out tonight."

If warnings like this were well received by old-timers, the new suburbanites looked at him in horror. So much so, he wondered what was wrong with people these days. Surely it couldn't just be television? Maybe it was all those other things too: computers, phones, headphones. So many people deaf to the world and everything in it. Meanwhile, standing there at the gate, he would receive news of old friends, living and dead.

Mr. Hicks gave much of their ample produce to remaining neighbors and friends, some of whom found themselves in a nearby residential home. When he gave them a cabbage or beetroot, their eyes brightened, and he was blithely unaware that none of these friends had their own cooking facilities; their meals prepared by staff who preferred the convenience of frozen food: diced vegetables, reconstituted mash. Visits to this place gave Mr. Hicks a queasy feeling of guilt and depression with, upon leaving, a sharp dose of euphoria. While too many of his contemporaries were moldering in armchairs, waiting for the Grim Reaper to cart them off, he was still enjoying life outdoors, tasting the sweet air, breathing in rich oxygen, taking every day as a gift that must not to be wasted.

With so many years gone, there were fewer old-timers passing by, and he found it odd, even dizzying, to find himself at an age where most people he'd known had moved into care or beyond that. Husbands were dutifully followed by wives into the great kingdom of God that Mr. Hicks felt certain was a magnificent vegetable garden, bathed in golden light.

Meanwhile, the old-timers in stout boots and thick caps were eclipsed by occasional joggers or young mothers with pushchairs who rarely said a word. He knew they were from across the way, where all the houses were the same. By night their illuminated windows glittered like fake jewels.

For all the plenitude of so much hard graft, the time and love spent toiling and tilling, there was no denying that for twenty years and more, *The Haven* had been under siege. Mr. Hicks had grown his hedges taller and thicker, but the traffic beyond had tripled. Twice a day, the tranquility of his garden was encircled with rush-hour anxiety and the curdling breath of its fumes. At the front, his laurel leaves were gray with dust and at the bottom of the garden, the housing estate had crept right up to the back of his fence. He could even watch people being murdered from his bedroom window! Across the way, a family was always watching a giant television at all times of the day and night. It disturbed him to be reminded that he and his wife were now surrounded by traffic islands and strangers, and what's more, strangers who liked to watch people murdering each other. Up until twenty years ago, life had been slow, steady, and *quiet*. But the years had concertinaed and unfolded, and slowly yet suddenly, it was all different now.

"*Oh!* That traffic!" Mrs. Hicks was vexed twice a day, and unlike her husband, was not the slightest bit deaf. It grew heavier; great juggernauts shook the house and there were more and more silver cars and dark-colored people carriers. Hairline cracks spread across their ceilings as proof. Mr. Hicks grew shy of standing at his gate; there were more people than he'd ever seen before, but he knew none of them, and very few would speak to him, even in long traffic jams with their windows down in summer. They preferred talking by phone as music belched from their cars, which were like beasts with great thudding hearts. Some of them pointed to his garden as if it was a tourist attraction, and they treated it like one, throwing crisp packets, bottles, and cans into it. Yet it seemed only yesterday that his garden had enjoyed the splendors of open privacy.

At last, walking around their garden one evening, surrounded by verdant foliage (such flowers and fruit!), Mr. and Mrs. Hicks talked of it at length. It was the longest conversation they'd had in years.

They prepared themselves.

Mr. Hicks observed the clouds' beautiful plumes and looked forward to being behind them; he hoped he'd be first and that his wife would soon join him. Mrs. Hicks hoped her husband went first so that he'd be waiting for her when she got there, just as he had at the crossroads on those summer evenings, to walk the lanes when they were young. Even though they knew the tide was coming in, they agreed they had so much to be grateful for. They still awoke to sweet birdsong, even if behind it, that rushing sound could never be mistaken for the sea.

From where he was standing during this conversation, Mr. Hicks could see the sun, gold and emerald on the underside of leaves, shimmering around the runner beans. They went into the house, where Mrs. Hicks had just finished making a new shirt for him and he had just repaired her shoes, one still upturned in a vice in the kitchen. They drank their tea and smiled because for most of the day and evening, silence still fell, and they were not like those other people who, said Mr. Hicks, might just as well have come from Mars.

Later that night, Mr. Hicks stepped into the spectral loneliness of the moonlight. He surveyed his garden, all so still and silent under the luminous moon, silvering the small lawn and gooseberry bush, the runner beans scaling their bamboo, the lettuces and carrot heads standing to attention like creatures large and small gathered for a grand occasion. Even in the moonlight, Mr. Hicks could feel the green of his garden, its richness and goodness surging in his bones, the sap rising. It was as if, like all his vegetation, fed and nourished by the peaty earth, he had taken root there. Tonight, the horse chestnut cast its great shadow over the entire garden, and its branches reached out to embrace all of it. In respect of its grandeur, Mr. Hicks removed his beret, stowed it in his pocket, and bowed. He walked further into the great chestnut's deepening shadow, and its branches rippled like reflections on water. He knew this tree's roots reached as far down into the earth, as the tree stood above it, arms out flung to a heaven hung with stars. Everything was in order, and knowing this, Mr. Hicks walked into the tumultuous embrace of the great tree, his spirit soaring, rising up faraway, like all lovely things faraway, the stars twinkling at the edge of his vision and reason.

Come morning, Mrs. Hicks saw that her lilies had bloomed overnight, so pale and white. These she arranged as calmly as usual. All was as silent as if snow had arrived, and she knew Mr. Hicks was where he wanted to be: in the garden where she would shortly join him. The best roses of the season were crimson and free of blight, and to celebrate this, she clipped them and wove them in her hair.

Red, pink, and white petals unfurled around her, and she knew the time had come.

AUTHOR BIOGRAPHIES

Jacquelyn Bengfort is a writer in Washington, DC. She used to drive warships around the world but she never met a merman (yet). Her fiction and essays have appeared in CHEAP POP, Tirage Monthly, Luna Luna, Storm Celler and elsewhere, and she can be found online at JaciB.com.

Susan Bianculli is a happily married mother of two living in Georgia who has loved to read all her life, and hopes to encourage children to the same love of reading she had at their age and still has today. You can learn more about her and her works on her website at susanbianculli.wix.com/home.

Chris Blocker holds an MFA in Writing from the University of Nebraska. His work has appeared in inscape and the Dia de los Muertos anthology. His novel, The Weeds Shall Inherit, is currently in revision. He lives in Topeka, Kansas.

Judi Calhoun is the author of Ancient Fire. Her short fiction has appeared in anthologies such as, Love Free or Die in the Granite State, Canopic Jars: Tales of Mummies & Mummification Bugs,Tales that Slither, Creep and Crawl, The Black Cat, and Motorcycle Anthology to name a few. She is currently working on a new novel, Dragon Girl.

Tara Campbell [www.taracampbell.com] is a Washington, D.C.-based writer of crossover sci-fi. With a BA in English and an MA in German Language and Literature, she has a demonstrated aversion to money and power. Her work has appeared in the Washington Independent Review of Books, Potomac Review Blog, Hogglepot Journal, Lorelei Signal, Punchnel's, GlassFire Magazine, the WiFiles, Silverthought Online, Toasted Cake Podcast, Litro Magazine, Luna Station Quarterly, Up Do: Flash Fiction by Women Writers, T. Gene Davis's Speculative Blog, Master's Review and Sci-Fi Romance Quarterly.

Frances Carden is currently pursuing her Master's degree in Writing at Johns Hopkins University. She has been published in Answers I'll Accept: True Accounts of Online dating, 20 Something Magazine, Wisteria Magazine, epinions.com, and is a writer at Readers Lane. She is currently working on a novel which takes place in the Democratic Republic of the Congo and Sudan.

Christina Elaine Collins is a Pushcart Prize-nominated fiction writer and an MFA candidate and teaching fellow at George Mason University. Her fiction can be found in literary periodicals such as Jabberwock Review, Weave Magazine, and NonBinary Review, as well as in anthologies from Tenebris Books and Fey Publishing. She's been an editor for So to Speak: A Feminist Journal of Language and Art, and as well a writer-in-residence at the Kimmel Harding Nelson Center for the Arts and the Art Commune program in Armenia.

Vonnie Winslow Crist is author of The Enchanted Skean (fantasy novel), Owl Light (speculative stories), The Greener Forest (fantasy stories), and other books. A clover-hand who's found so many four-leafed clovers that she keeps them in jars, Vonnie believes the world is filled with mystery, miracles, and magic.

An award-winning scientist and author, **Arthur M. Doweyko** enjoys the challenge of crafting convincing science fiction. His short stories which have garnered numerous honors have appeared in a number of anthologies and his debut novel, Algorithm, will be published by E-Lit Books in October, 2014. He jousts with aliens from other worlds, while teaching college chemistry and living in Florida with his wife, Lidia.

Oliver Gray was raised in the suburbs of Maryland, and earned his M.A. from The Johns Hopkins University. His essays and stories have been published in the Tin House, Good Men Project, The TJ Eckleberg Review, 20 Something Magazine, and Outside In Literary and Travel Magazine. His beer and writing blog, Literature and Libation, won the North American Guild of Beer Writers' "Blog of the Year" award in 2013. He currently lives just outside of Washington DC and is working on a beer and brewing themed book.

Helen Grochmal started writing fiction in her 60s when she moved to a retirement home with her cat. She has had two mysteries published by Cozy Cat Press (one in process) and has started experimenting with writing short forms of all sorts with some success.

Misha Herwin is a writer of books and short stories for adults, children and YAs. She is fascinated by time and loves creating alternative, magical worlds. In her spare time she is either reading, or baking, muffins are a speciality.

Paul Houghton is a fiction writer who has published stories in UK magazines and anthologies such as: Mouth, The Fiction Magazine, Panurge, Gutter and You Are Here: an anthology of British Stories edited by Bill Broady. He has also made short films which have been shown at the

Institute of Contemporary Art (London) and on Scottish TV. He studied creative writing at UEA under Angela Carter and is currently a Senior Lecturer in Creative Writing at Staffordshire University, England.

The short stories of Brooklyn-based author **Anne E. Johnson** have appeared in FrostFire Worlds, Shelter of Daylight, The Future Fire, Liquid Imagination, and elsewhere. Her series of humorous science fiction novels, The Webrid Chronicles, is being published by Candlemark & Gleam. Learn about Anne's work, including her speculative fiction for children and tweens, on her website, http://anneejohnson.com.

Aline Boucher Kaplan has been writing science fiction since 1980 and has published two novels, both through Baen books, as well as about two dozen short stories and one novella. She has been a member of the Science Fiction and Fantasy Writers of America (SFWA) since 1989. For at least 15 years she has participated in the SpaceCrafts writing group, which focuses on reading and critiquing science fiction and fantasy work.

Christina Marie Keller lives and works in the Washington, DC area. She is currently pursuing her master's degree at Johns Hopkins University. For more information, please visit her blog, which can be found at www.christinamarieblog.wordpress.com.

Born and raised in Northern California, **Jessica Knauss** is a New Englander by design. She has published fiction, poetry, and nonfiction in numerous venues, including Bewildering Stories, Do Not Look at the Sun, (Short) Fiction Collective, Full of Crow Quarterly Fiction, Metazen, and Short, Fast, and Deadly. Get updates on her writing at her blog: jessicaknauss.blogspot.com.

Llanwyre Laish's formative years were filled with the fairy tales and myths of Britain and Ireland. As an adult, she spent nine years sandwiched between gargoyles and rare books, racking up degrees while studying the versions of those tales told in the Middle Ages and the nineteenth century. She now teaches academic writing and writes about roleplaying games.

Elizabeth Nellums is an aspiring mystery novelist who lives and works in Washington DC. She also writes short stories in a variety of genres, often focusing on rural or agricultural themes.

T.A. Noonan is the author of several books and chapbooks, most recently four sparks fall: a novella (Chicago Center for Literature and Photography, 2013) and, with Erin Elizabeth Smith, Skate or Die (Dusie

Kollktiv, 2014). Her work has appeared or is forthcoming in Reunion: The Dallas Review, Menacing Hedge, LIT, West Wind Review, Ninth Letter, Phoebe, and many others. A weightlifter, crafter, priestess, and all-around woman of action.

Helen Ogden is a 34 year old UK born writer of speculative fantasy poetry, prose and children's stories. Her work has appeared in Goblin Fruit, Cabinet Des Fees, Jabberwocky Magazine, Mirror Dance and Cinnamon Press anthology In The Telling. She has also received honorable mentions from respected editor Ellen Datlow for her work.

David Perlmutter is a freelance writer based in Winnipeg, Manitoba, Canada. The holder of an MA degree from the Universities of Manitoba and Winnipeg, and a lifelong animation fan, he has published short fiction in a variety of genres for various magazines and anthologies, as well as essays on his favorite topics for similar publishers. He is the author of America Toons In: A History of Television Animation (McFarland and Co.), The Singular Adventures Of Jefferson Ball (Chupa Cabra Press) and The Pups (Booklocker.com).

Constance Renfrow is an editor at Three Rooms Press; an editorial and publishing consultant at constancerenfrow.com; and the graphic designer for the Merchant's House Museum. Her work is forthcoming in Petrichor Machine and has been featured in Two Cities Review, Rapportage, and CityElla. She is absolutely in love with the Victorian era, so she's naturally working on her three-volume novel, when she's not blogging at 21stcenturyvictorian.com.

Katherine Sanger was a Jersey Girl before getting smart and moving to Texas. She's been published in various e-zines and print, including Baen's Universe, Black Chaos, Wandering Weeds, Spacesports & Spidersilk, Black Petals, Star*Line, Anotherealm, Lost in the Dark, Bewildering Stories, Aphelion, and RevolutionSF, edited From the Asylum, an e-zine of fiction and poetry, and is the current editor of "Serial Flasher," a twitter-zine. She's a member of HWA and SFWA. She taught English for over 10 years at various online and local community and technical colleges.

Melody Schreiber is a program manager at the International Reporting Project and a freelance writer based in Washington, D.C. Her short stories, essays, articles, and reviews have been published by District Lines, The Washington Post, Maryland Life, Slate, and others. Follow her on Twitter and Instagram, where she takes too many photos of her pets and favorite books, at @m_scribe.

Stefen Styrsky's poetry and stories have appeared in Cactus Heart, The James White Review, Between, New Voices in Gay Fiction, Best Gay Stories 2014, and The Tahoma Literary Review. He is one thesis class away from receiving his MA in Fiction Writing from the Johns Hopkins University. He lives in Washington, DC.

Jake Teeny graduated from Santa Clara University with a dual degree in philosophy and psychology and now attends Ohio State University for a doctorate in social psychology. When not conducting research, he loves to write fiction, box competitively, and list items in groups of threes. A list of his published work as well as his weekly blog, "Psychophilosophy tips for everyday living" can be found at www.jaketeeny.com.

Tim Tobin holds a degree in mathematics from LaSalle University and is retired from L-3 Communications. He and his wife MaryAnn live in New Jersey and have two daughters and the joy of their lives, a seven year-old grandson and a three-year old granddaughter. His work appears in Grey Wolfe Press, In Parentheses, River Poets Journal, Static Movement, Cruentus Libri Press, The Speculative Edge, Rainstorm Press, Twisted Dreams, The Rusty Nail, Whortleberry Press and various websites and ezines.

Angeline Trevena is a horror and fantasy writer from Devon, UK, where she lives above a milkshake shop. Some years ago she worked at an antique auction house and religiously checked every wardrobe that came in to see if Narnia was in the back of it. She's still not given up looking for it.

Carmen Tudor writes adult and YA spec fic from Melbourne, Australia. Catch her latest stories in Fantasy For Good, Tales of Mystery, Suspense & Terror, and Miseria's Chorale. You can find Carmen online at carmentudor.net and tweeting under @carmen_tudor.

Clint Wastling is a writer based in the East Riding of Yorkshire. His stories have appeared in anthologies in the USA and UK recently: Pressed by Unseen Feet and Contact: Stories of the New World as well as numerous magazines. His novel, The Geology of Desire, will be published by Stairwell Books in September 2014. Further information at www.clintwastling.webs.com.

ABOUT THE EDITOR

Kelly Ann Jacobson is a fiction writer, poet, and lyricist who lives in Falls Church, Virginia. She recently received her MA in Fiction at Johns Hopkins University, and she now teaches as a Professor of Literature and a Writing Lab Instructor. Kelly is the author of the literary fiction novel *Cairo in White* and the young adult trilogy *The Zaniyah Trilogy*, as well as the editor of the book of essays *Answers I'll Accept: True Accounts of Online Dating*. Her work, including her published poems, fiction, lyrics, and nonfiction, can be found at www.kellyannjacobson.com.

Made in the USA
San Bernardino, CA
13 November 2014